Hands-On Microsoft Teams

A practical guide to enhancing enterprise collaboration with Microsoft Teams and Office 365

João Ferreira

BIRMINGHAM—MUMBAI

Hands-On Microsoft Teams

Commissioning Editor: Pavan Ramchandani
Acquisition Editor: Pavan Ramchandani
Senior Editor: Hayden Edwards
Content Development Editor: Keagan Carneiro
Technical Editor: Deepesh Patel
Copy Editor: Safis Editing
Project Coordinator: Kinjal Bari
Proofreader: Safis Editing
Indexer: Tejal Daruwale Soni
Production Designer: Alishon Mendonsa

First published: April 2020

Production reference: 1290420

Published by Packt Publishing Ltd.
Livery Place
35 Livery Street
Birmingham
B3 2PB, UK.

ISBN 978-1-83921-398-4

Packt.com

To my mother, Maria José Oliveira, and my father, Carlos Ferreira, for their constant support.

– João Carlos Oliveira Ferreira

Packt.com

Subscribe to our online digital library for full access to over 7,000 books and videos, as well as industry leading tools to help you plan your personal development and advance your career. For more information, please visit our website.

Why subscribe?

- Spend less time learning and more time coding with practical eBooks and videos from over 4,000 industry professionals

- Improve your learning with skill plans designed especially for you

- Get a free eBook or video every month

- Fully searchable for easy access to vital information

- Copy and paste, print, and bookmark content

Did you know that Packt offers eBook versions of every book published, with PDF and ePub files available? You can upgrade to the eBook version at packt.com and, as a print book customer, you are entitled to a discount on the eBook copy. Get in touch with us at customercare@packtpub.com for more details.

At www.packt.com, you can also read a collection of free technical articles, sign up for a range of free newsletters, and receive exclusive discounts and offers on Packt books and eBooks.

Contributors

About the author

João Carlos Oliveira Ferreira is an acclaimed Microsoft MVP, MCP, and MCSA. João has been working with SharePoint for the last 8 years and embraced Microsoft Teams right from day one. João is responsible for the development of several products and is also the manager of several development teams.

> When I was a child, I always dreamed of writing a book. Years passed by and this idea was forgotten, until the day Packt reached out to me to write this book.
>
> None of this would have been possible without the support of my family, my girlfriend, and my friends, who gave me confidence and helped me to keep up the writing pace.
>
> Thanks to everyone at Packt who taught me so much about the book-writing process and offered valuable suggestions that ultimately will make you a Microsoft Teams hero.
>
> Lastly, I want to thank the Microsoft community for always being willing to help others.

About the reviewer

Michael LaMontagne is a Microsoft solutions advisor, partner evangelist, and six-time Microsoft MVP for Office Apps and Services. Michael runs the Calgary **Unified Communications (UC)** Users Group and is a member of the O365Eh! podcast.

Michael's focus is bridging professional services, products, and innovation, while working closely with Microsoft's product groups via **Technology Adoption Programs (TAPs)** as well as the MVP, DnA, and Elite programs. In his spare time, Michael dabbles in development around Azure services, bots, the Internet of Things, Microsoft Graph, Microsoft Power Automate, and PowerShell, and he is a father of three children under seven.

Packt is searching for authors like you

If you're interested in becoming an author for Packt, please visit `authors.packtpub.com` and apply today. We have worked with thousands of developers and tech professionals, just like you, to help them share their insight with the global tech community. You can make a general application, apply for a specific hot topic that we are recruiting an author for, or submit your own idea.

Table of Contents

3

How to Use Microsoft Teams – Chats and Conversation

4

How to Use Microsoft Teams – Meetings and Live Events

5

Public versus Private – Teams and Channels

6

Extending Microsoft Teams Using Apps

7

Extend Microsoft Teams Using Custom Apps and Microsoft 365

8

Build Your Own App for Microsoft Teams Using App Studio

9

Building Your Own Bot for Microsoft Teams

10

Microsoft Teams PowerShell – a Tool for Automation

Other Books You May Enjoy

Preface

Microsoft Teams, released in 2017, is a communication platform that evolved from Microsoft's Skype for Business. In a single platform, Teams integrates most of the services included in Microsoft 365 and offers the perfect solution for chat, video calling, and file storage while still providing extensibility endpoints that allow anyone to build business processes and applications inside Microsoft Teams.

Who this book is for

This Microsoft Teams book is for power users and business professionals looking to use Teams to improve collaboration in an enterprise environment. It will also be useful to Office 365 administrators interested in implementing Microsoft Teams effectively by gaining knowledge and picking up expert tips and best practices to ensure good governance.

What this book covers

Chapter 1, *Microsoft Teams Basics*, enumerates each individual element of Microsoft Teams. These are the key concepts that you need to get to grips with in order to understand how to use the platform. The chapter also explains what other platforms from Microsoft 365 are used when a team is created in Teams. This helps you understand how things are connected inside the Microsoft ecosystem and how they are exposed and made available in a single location inside Microsoft Teams.

Chapter 2, *Microsoft Teams' Core Features*, covers all the default features that exist in Microsoft Teams out of the box. It provides a detailed explanation of all the features, including search, filters, commands, and the calendar, and explains where the data generated by each of the features is stored.

Chapter 3, *How to Use Microsoft Teams – Chats and Conversation*, explains the base features that make Microsoft Teams one of the best collaboration platforms o n the market. It goes through all the details associated with the chat feature for 1:1 and team chats.

Chapter 4, How to Use Microsoft Teams – Meetings and Live Events, covers meeting functionalities in detail, from scheduling meetings to sharing screens. It also gets into the admin options for enabling meeting features for guest users, such as remote control during a meeting.

Chapter 5, Public versus Private – Teams and Channels, covers teams and channels and the levels of privacy that can be defined for each. It highlights the differences between public and private channels and dives into the details of the architecture with scenarios that help you to understand when to use various channels.

Chapter 6, Extending Microsoft Teams Using Apps, introduces Microsoft Teams apps and teaches you how the platform can be extended using the five different types of apps.

Chapter 7, Extend Microsoft Teams Using Custom Apps and Microsoft 365, looks at custom apps. Even though Microsoft Teams offers an app store to extend the platform, it will probably not be enough for most businesses. Large organizations each have their own business processes that won't be catered for exactly by standard products. This chapter guides you on how to enable and install custom apps on Microsoft Teams.

Chapter 8, Build Your Own App for Microsoft Teams Using App Studio, covers Microsoft Teams App Studio, a "development" app that empowers any end user to build their own custom apps directly inside Microsoft Teams.

Chapter 9, Building Your Own Bot for Microsoft Teams, covers the creation of bots, powerful automated agents that will help you to accomplish daily tasks in an efficient way using natural language. Even though it sounds futuristic and complex, building a bot is accessible to everyone and does not require code. This chapter includes a step-by-step guide to creating and deploying a bot on Microsoft Teams.

Chapter 10, Microsoft Teams PowerShell – a Tool for Automation, explores PowerShell. Microsoft Teams admins will end up doing repetitive tasks to create and configure teams; this chapter introduces the PowerShell modules available for the platform that allow the automation of tasks.

To get the most out of this book

To get the most out of this book, you should have a Microsoft Teams account (free or business) and you should have the application installed on your computer and mobile phones.

The final chapter of the book covers the use of PowerShell, which requires the installation of the Microsoft Teams and Skype for Business modules. It's assumed that you are familiar with basic programming concepts.

Software covered in the book	OS requirements
Microsoft Teams	Windows, macOS X, or Linux Android or iOS
Microsoft Teams PowerShell module	Windows
Skype for Business PowerShell module	Windows

If you are using the digital version of this book, we advise you to type the code yourself or access the code via the GitHub repository (link available in the next section). Doing so will help you avoid any potential errors related to the copying/pasting of code.

Download the example code files

You can download the example code files for this book from your account at www. packt.com. If you purchased this book elsewhere, you can visit www.packt.com/support and register to have the files emailed directly to you.

You can download the code files by following these steps:

1. Log in or register at www.packt.com.
2. Select the **Support** tab.
3. Click on **Code Downloads**.
4. Enter the name of the book in the **Search** box and follow the onscreen instructions.

Once the file is downloaded, please make sure that you unzip or extract the folder using the latest version of:

- WinRAR/7-Zip for Windows
- Zipeg/iZip/UnRarX for Mac
- 7-Zip/PeaZip for Linux

The code bundle for the book is also hosted on GitHub at https://github.com/PacktPublishing/-Hands-On-Microsoft-Teams. In case there's an update to the code, it will be updated on the existing GitHub repository.

We also have other code bundles from our rich catalog of books and videos available at https://github.com/PacktPublishing/. Check them out!

Conventions used

There are a number of text conventions used throughout this book.

Bold: Indicates a new term, an important word, or words that you see on screen. For example, words in menus or dialog boxes appear in the text like this. Here is an example: "Select **System info** from the **Administration** panel."

> Tips, important notes or scenarios
> appear like this.

A block of code is set as follows:

```
$teamName= "Project Y"
$teamDescription= "The new generation of electric skateboards"
$teamOwner= "joao@funskating.com"
$teamVisibility= "Private"
$teamEditMessagesPolicy= $false
$teamDeliteMessagesPolicy= $false
```

Get in touch

Feedback from our readers is always welcome.

General feedback: If you have questions about any aspect of this book, mention the book title in the subject of your message and email us at customercare@packtpub.com.

Errata: Although we have taken every care to ensure the accuracy of our content, mistakes do happen. If you have found a mistake in this book, we would be grateful if you would report this to us. Please visit www.packtpub.com/support/errata, selecting your book, clicking on the Errata Submission Form link, and entering the details.

Piracy: If you come across any illegal copies of our works in any form on the internet, we would be grateful if you would provide us with the location address or website name. Please contact us at copyright@packt.com with a link to the material.

If you are interested in becoming an author: If there is a topic that you have expertise in, and you are interested in either writing or contributing to a book, please visit authors. packtpub.com.

Reviews

Please leave a review. Once you have read and used this book, why not leave a review on the site that you purchased it from? Potential readers can then see and use your unbiased opinion to make purchase decisions, we at Packt can understand what you think about our products, and our authors can see your feedback on their book. Thank you!

For more information about Packt, please visit packt.com.

1
Microsoft Teams Basics

Microsoft Teams is a new collaboration tool that is transforming the way people work and collaborate around the world. It reached more than 44 million active users in 2020 Q1 and does not show any signs of slowing down.

Workers spend part of their day switching between platforms to chat with their peers, access the project's documentation, schedule meetings, share files, and more. All of these tasks can be finally centralized in a single workspace, and that workspace is Microsoft Teams.

Microsoft has a lot of experience with communication and collaboration tools and Microsoft Teams is an evolution of their previous solutions. Teams inherits all the experience and know-how acquired from other Microsoft enterprise solutions over the last 20 years and is the natural successor of Microsoft Lync and Skype for Business.

If you are reading this book, you have probably asked yourself – Why Microsoft Teams?

Microsoft Teams connects the dots between other Microsoft services and applications used in business environments, empowers users to achieve more, reduces the associated costs, and boosts employee engagement.

If you want to embrace the modern workplace journey and give your teams a boost using Microsoft Teams, this book is for you.

In this chapter, we are going to cover the following topics:

- Accessing Microsoft Teams
- How to sign in on Microsoft Teams
- What does Microsoft Teams look like?
- What is a team?
- What is a channel?
- What is a tab?

Accessing Microsoft Teams

First things first, before we start digging into Microsoft Teams concepts, you need to know how and where you can access it so that you can begin working with Teams right away.

Microsoft Teams plans

Microsoft Teams has two different plans: a free version that is available for anyone to use and a paid version that is included in the Office 365 Business plans.

If you do not have access to an Office 365 subscription and still want to implement Microsoft Teams, you can start with the free version, but be aware of its limitations. The following table shows a comparison between the free and paid versions that might help you decide which version suits your needs:

	Free	Office 365 Business
Unlimited Messages and Chat	Yes	Yes
Guest Access	Yes	Yes
Maximum Users	300	Unlimited *associated with the number of Office 365 licenses
Online Video and Audio Calls	Yes	Yes
Schedule Meetings	No	Yes
Meeting Recordings	No	Yes
File Storage	2 GB/User 10 GB of shared storage	1 TB/User
Multifactor Authentication	No	Yes
Support	No	Yes

As you can see, the free version of Microsoft Teams has some limitations and it might not suit all scenarios. However, if you are building a proof of concept to drive the adoption of the platform, it can be a starting point. A detailed and updated comparison of all the Teams versions can be found online at `https://products.office.com/en/microsoft-teams/free`.

Microsoft Teams clients

To get started with Microsoft Teams, first, you need to know how to access it.

Teams is available for a variety of platforms. You can use it through any of the following:

- A web browser
- A desktop application
- A mobile application

Each version has its own specifications and features, so be aware that your experience of Teams might be different if you're using it on multiple devices. To get the best experience while using Microsoft Teams, it's recommended to use the native clients for mobile and desktop.

Web clients

Microsoft Teams is available as a web app and can be accessed directly from a browser by going to `https://teams.microsoft.com`. The web version allows you to use the main functionalities of Microsoft Teams, but you might face some limitations, depending on the browser you are using:

	Calls			Meetings		
	Audio	Video	Sharing	Audio	Video	Sharing
Internet Explorer 11	✗	✗	✗	*	✗	*1
Edge RS2	✓	✓	*1	✓	✓	*1
Edge (Chromium)	✓	✓	✓	✓	✓	✓
Google Chrome	✓	✓	✓	✓	✓	✓
Firefox	✗	✗	✗	*	✗	*1
Safari 11.1+	✗	✗	✗	*	✗	*1

*PSTN coordinates are required to attend the meeting.

*1Incoming sharing only.

When accessing the Microsoft Teams web app for the first time, you will have to bypass the download app screen by clicking the **Use web app instead** link:

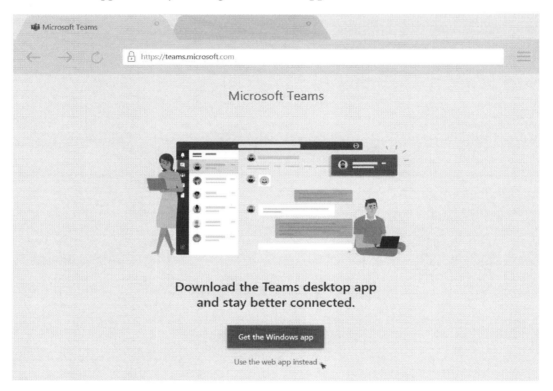

Figure 1.1: Selecting the web app

If your browser is not compatible with the web version of Microsoft Teams, access to the app will be blocked and you will see a message asking you to download the app for your operating system.

Desktop clients

The full-feature experience of Microsoft Teams can be only achieved when using the desktop clients available for Windows, macOS, and Linux.

The Microsoft Teams client for Windows supports 32-bit and 64-bit architectures; unlike other office apps, it is agnostic of the architecture of the version of Microsoft Office you have installed and does not require administrator privileges to be installed. This is because the application is deployed in the user's profile folder, that is, AppData.

To install Microsoft Teams on Windows, you need to have the minimum requirements listed in the following table:

Component	Requirements
Processor	Minimum 1.6 GHz, 32-bit or 64-bit
Memory RAM	2.0 GB (4 GB is recommended for live events)
GPU	128 MB
Disk Space	3 GB available
Screen	1,024 x 768 or higher
Operating System	Windows 10, Windows 8.1
Devices	Camera, microphone, speakers

macOS

The Microsoft Teams client for macOS is available as a PKG installation file and requires administrator privileges to be installed; the application is deployed to the /Application folder.

To install Microsoft Teams on macOS, you need to have the minimum requirements listed in the following table:

Component	Requirements
Processor	Intel Core 2 Duo or higher
Memory RAM	2.0 GB (4 GB is recommended for live events)
Disk Space	1.5 GB available
Screen	1,280 x 800 or higher
Operating System	macOS X 10.11 El Capitan or higher
Devices	Camera, microphone, speakers

Linux

The Microsoft Teams client for Linux is available for Debian distributions and for Red Hat-based distributions. The installation packages are provided in DEB format (for Debian) and RPM format (for Red Hat).

Linux has a lot of different distributions but among the most used ones are Ubuntu, which are based on the Debian distribution package, and CentOS and Fedora, which are based on the Red Hat distribution package.

To install Microsoft Teams on Linux, you need to have the minimum requirements listed in the following table:

Component	Requirements
Processor	Intel Core 2 duo or higher
Memory RAM	2.0 GB (4 GB is recommended for live events)
GPU	128 MB
Disk Space	3 GB available
Screen	1,024 x 768 or higher
Operating System	Ubuntu 16.04 LTS or higher LTS version, CentOS 8, Fedora 30, RHEL 8
Devices	Camera, microphone, speakers

Mobile clients

As a platform that aims to facilitate communication and collaboration in the modern workplace environment, Microsoft Teams is also available for Android and iOS.

Android

The Android version of Microsoft Teams is available for download on the Google Play Store and is compatible with the last four major versions of Android.

For example, at the time of writing, Android is on version 10, which means that Microsoft Teams is officially supported on Android 7 or higher.

Depending on the evolution of the Android operating system, the support for Microsoft Teams can be extended to older versions. To find out what the latest version supported is, you can check the requirements for Microsoft Teams on the Google Play Store.

iOS

The iOS version of Microsoft Teams is available for download on the Apple App Store and is compatible with the last two major versions of iOS. Microsoft Teams is compatible with all iOS devices, including iPhone, iPad, and iPod Touch.

For example, iOS is on version 13, which means that Microsoft Teams is officially supported on iOS 11 or higher.

Depending on the evolution of the iOS operating system, the support for Microsoft Teams can be extended to older versions. To find out what the latest version support is, you can check the requirements for Microsoft Teams on the Apple App Store.

How to sign in to Microsoft Teams

After installing Microsoft Teams, you will need to sign in to the application. You can do this using your work, school, or Microsoft account.

When you first open the Microsoft Teams application, you will be asked for your email, as shown in the following screenshot. Once you've typed in your email, click on **Sign in**. When you do this, the application will request your password:

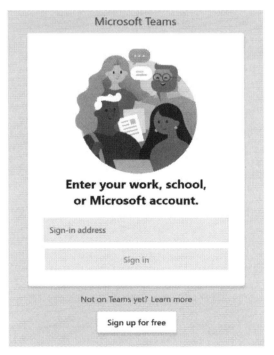

Figure 1.2: Sign in window when using the Microsoft Teams client

After providing your credentials, the application will take a few seconds to load all your teams and conversations. Then, you will be ready to communicate with your colleagues.

When using the web version of Microsoft Teams, the sign-in process is a bit different. The first thing you need to do is type `https://teams.microsoft.com` into the address bar of your browser.

If you are not authenticated with your email account for any Microsoft service, you will be redirected to the default federation authentication page, which looks as follows:

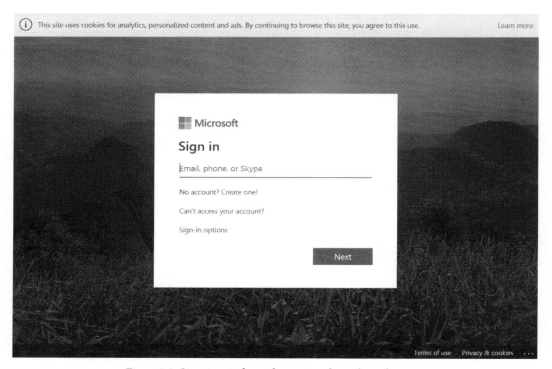

Figure1.3: Sign-in window when using the web application

You will need to provide your email and click on **Next**. After doing that, provide your password and click on **Sign in**.

Like the desktop client, the application only takes a few seconds to load after a successful sign in.

The sign-in process in the mobile client is fairly similar and you will need to provide your email and password to go through the authentication process.

What does Microsoft Teams look like?

Now that you have Microsoft Teams installed on one or more devices, it is time to take a look at the application layout and learn how it is organized.

The following screenshot represents the web or desktop version of Microsoft Teams. All the major components are identified with numbers:

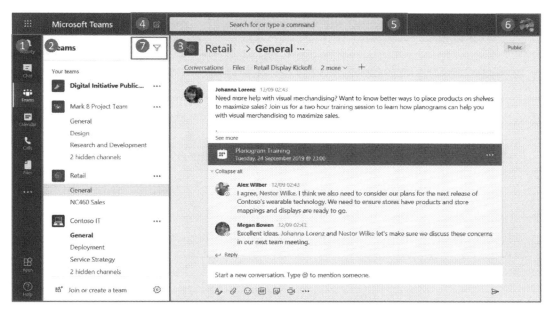

Figure 1.4: Main window of Microsoft Teams

Let's take a look at the different components, all of which have been numbered in the preceding screenshot:

1. **App bar**: By default, the app bar shows **Activity, Chat, Teams, Calendar, Calls,** and **Files**. These are the main default features of Microsoft Teams. This bar can be customized, and a Microsoft Teams administrator can add more apps to it and define the position of new apps. However, the default apps cannot be removed. If a new app is added to the first six positions, the default app is moved to the submenu, which can be accessed through the ... icon.

2. **Left pane**: The context of the left pane changes according to the app that is selected. From this pane, you can access your contacts, chats, and teams. The left pane is not used by all Microsoft Teams apps; apps such as the calendar only make use of the stage section.

3. **Stage**: The stage is where the main content of the app is displayed. It is from this section that you will chat with your colleagues and send or download files, among other things.

4. **New Chat**: This button allows you to start a new conversation with one user or with multiple users. The conversations will then appear in the Chat app.

5. **Search and Commands**: The search box has two functionalities built into it. It allows you to perform a global search on Microsoft Teams for files, people, and messages and also allows you to use commands to perform common tasks. To use a command, type / into the text box and choose a command from the list.

6. **Profile and settings**: Your avatar allows access to personal settings. From this option, you will be able to change your current status, which indicates your availability. It also allows you to access your saved messages and configure the global options of the Microsoft Teams app.

7. **Filters**: The filter option works in the context of the app you have selected, and it will show the results in the left pane.

Microsoft Teams is also available for mobile devices, but because of the smaller screen size, the app's layout is different. Not all desktop features are available in the mobile version, though Microsoft is adding them gradually to mobile apps. The following screenshot represents the mobile version of Microsoft Teams. All the main components are identified with numbers:

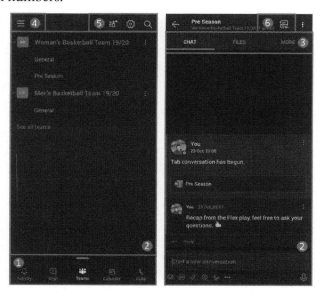

Figure 1.5: Microsoft Teams mobile layout

Let's take a look at the different components, all of which have been numbered in the preceding screenshot:

1. **App bar**: By default, the app bar shows **Activity, Chat, Teams, Calendar, Calls,** and these apps cannot be modified. To view the other apps, you need to swipe the app bar up and the app icons will appear inside a panel.

2. **Stage**: The stage on mobile displays the information from the desktop left pane and from the stage area. The stage has several levels and allows you navigate inside of your teams or chats.

3. **Tab**: By default, the app shows the **Chat** and **Files** tabs. Any other tabs that exist in the channel are displayed when you click on **More**.

4. **Menu**: The menu allows you to access the personal settings. From here, you will be able to change your current status, which indicates your availability. It also allows you to access your saved messages and configure the global options of the Microsoft Teams app. From the menu, you can also select all the tenants where you logged on to Microsoft Teams. This option allows you to switch between organizations and currently is only available on the mobile app.

5. **Search and tools**: The search icon a magnifying glass, allows you to search globally in the Microsoft Teams app. The cog icon allows you to select the Teams you want to see by default, while the + icon allows you to join or create a team.

6. **Follow channel**: This option allows you to receive notifications from the channels you follow to avoid losing important information.

Now that you are familiar with the look of Microsoft Teams on desktop and mobile, it's time to understand its main components as explained in the following sections.

What is a team?

A team is a group of people that can represent a department, a project, a class, or even a sports team. Besides grouping people, Teams also gathers a set of tools that allows members to share information and work together.

The following scenarios will be used to explain the ways you can tailor team creation for a specific team's requirements. I've tried to add as many examples as possible from multiple sectors, even though they may not fit in the overall setup of the book, just so that you are be able to connect these scenarios with your own realities.

Team Scenario #1 –Mary the marketing manager

Mary is the marketing manager for a multinational company leading a global marketing team currently working on a worldwide campaign for the holidays. Mary has created a team in Microsoft Teams that allows her to do the following:

• Keep conversations about the campaign with other members of the marketing department.

• Share documents about the campaign.

• Invite guest members to the team who will produce the TV commercials to keep them updated with the campaign ideas.

• Access the campaign tasks to each member.

Team Scenario #2 – Geno the basketball coach

Geno is a college basketball coach preparing for a new season. As the head coach, he wants to make communicating and sharing information between team members easier.

Geno has decided to create a team on Microsoft Teams that allows him to do the following:

• Keep all the team members, players, coaches, and physical therapists in communication with each other on the same channel.

• Schedule practices.

• Share the games calendar.

• Share the results from other teams and the standings.

• Share scouting videos.

Creating a new team

Creating a new team is the first step to taking advantage of the collaborative features Microsoft Teams offers. This can be done from all app types, although the options might appear in different locations, depending on the operating system you're using.

To create a new empty team using the web or desktop version of Microsoft Teams, do the following:

1. Open the Microsoft Teams App.

2. On the app bar, click on **Teams**.

3. Click on **Join or create a team** or click on the **Create a team** tile, as shown in the following screenshot:

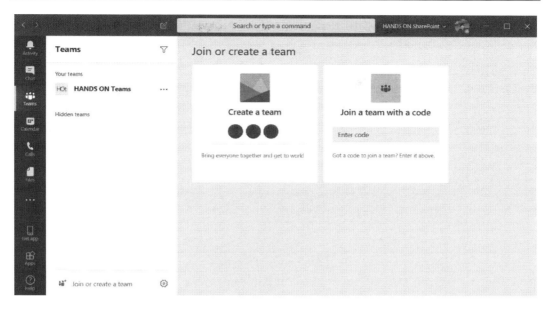

Figure 1.6: Join or create a team

4. On the **Create your team** popup, you can choose between the options shown in the following screenshot:

Figure 1.7: Create team options

Let's explain these options in more detail:

(a) Build a team from scratch: This option will create an empty team with a chat, a document library, and a wiki.

(b) Create from an existing Office 365 group or team: This option allows you to create a team from an existing Office 365 group or use an existing team as a template for your new team.

5. As a team owner, you can choose from three different levels of privacy for the team, as shown in the following screenshot:

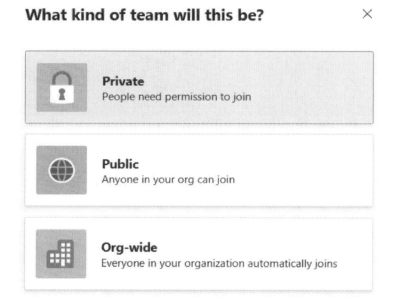

Figure 1.8: Privacy selection

Let's explain these options in more detail:

(a) Private: People need to be added by a team owner and the team cannot be discovered on the Microsoft Teams app by default.

(b) Public: Anyone in the organization can join and the team can be discovered through the Microsoft Teams app.

(c) Org-Wide: Everyone in the organization is added to the team automatically and is kept in sync with the Active Directory as more users join or leave the organization. This option is only available for environments with less than 5,000 users and only global admins will be able to create org-wide teams.

6.   Provide a name and a description for your team and click the **Create** button:

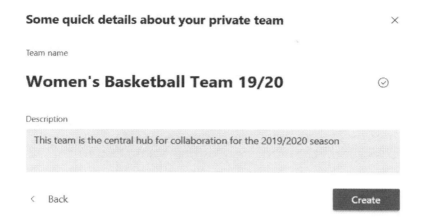

Figure 1.9: Team name and description

7.   Wait a few seconds for the success message to appear. Now, you are ready to start adding members to your newly created team.

If your organization is already using Office 365 groups and you want to create a team out of it or you want to use an existing team as a template for your new team, do the following:

1.   Follow the preceding steps until *step 4.*

2.   Select **Create from an existing Office 365 group or team**.

3.   Select either **Team** or **Office 365 group**. Both options will show you a list of the teams or groups that you have access to:

Figure 1.10: Create team from existing content

4. Pick the desired team or group:

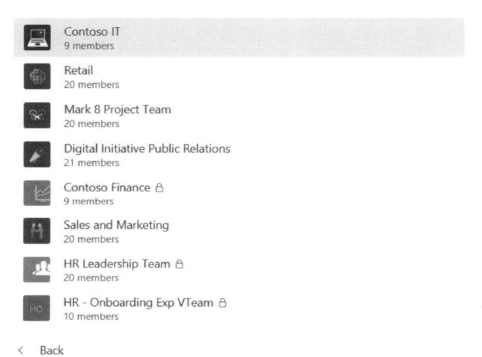

Which team do you want to use?   ✕

Copy apps, settings, and channels over to your new team. Your existing team won't be changed.

Contoso IT
9 members

Retail
20 members

Mark 8 Project Team
20 members

Digital Initiative Public Relations
21 members

Contoso Finance 🔒
9 members

Sales and Marketing
20 members

HR Leadership Team 🔒
20 members

HR - Onboarding Exp VTeam 🔒
10 members

‹   Back

Figure 1.11: Team selection

5. When a new team is created from an existing team, you will have the option to control everything that is related to it. This includes the following:

    (a) **Name**

    (b) **Description**

    (c) **Privacy**

    (d) **Members**

    (e) **Tabs**

    (f) **Channels**

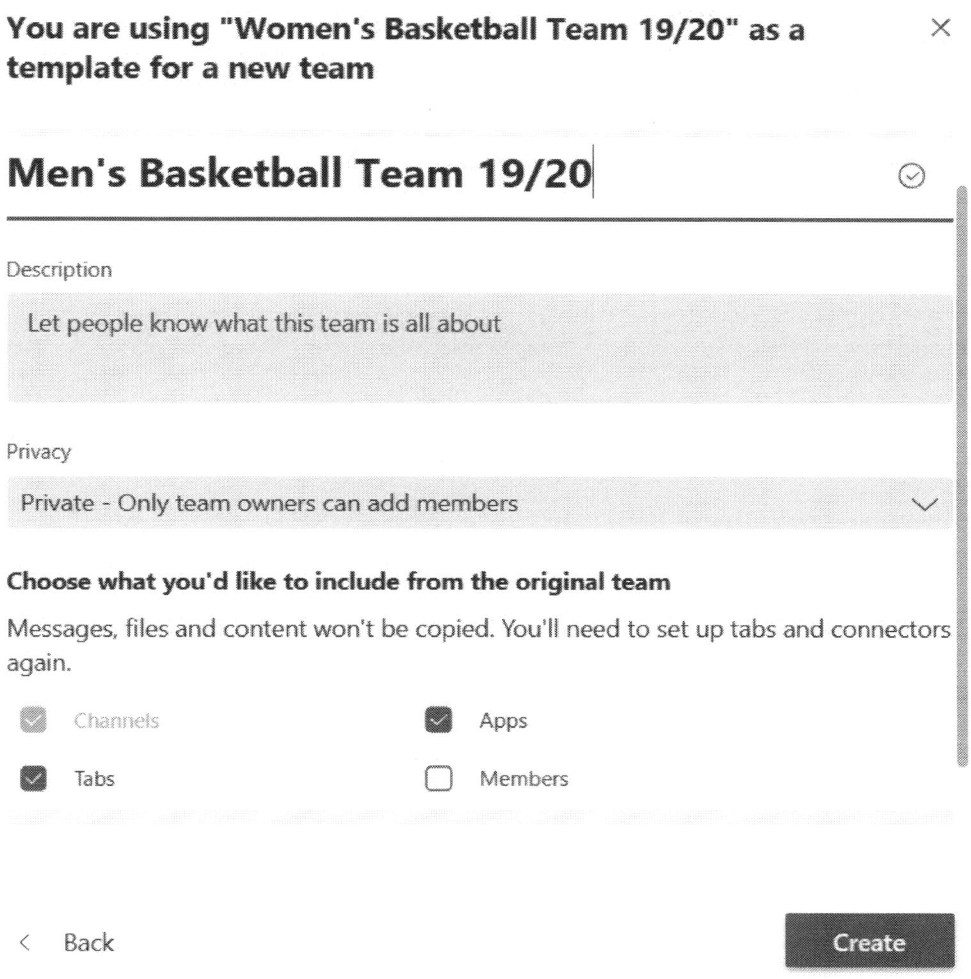

You are using "Women's Basketball Team 19/20" as a   ✕
template for a new team

Men's Basketball Team 19/20   ⊘

Description

Let people know what this team is all about

Privacy

Private - Only team owners can add members   ⌄

Choose what you'd like to include from the original team

Messages, files and content won't be copied. You'll need to set up tabs and connectors again.

☑ Channels   ☑ Apps

☑ Tabs   ☐ Members

‹ Back   Create

Figure 1.12: Create new team from template

6. When a new team is created from Office 365 groups, it inherits the settings from the group, namely the following:

    (a) Name

    (b) Description

    (c) Privacy

    (d) Members

7. Click the **Create** button. Now, you are ready to start using your new team.

What happens when I create a team?

Microsoft Teams is tightly connected to other Office 365 applications and makes use of some of them to provide a rich collaboration environment every time a new team is created. The following are created when you create a team:

- A new Office 365 group
- A SharePoint site collection
- A shared calendar and a shared mailbox
- A OneNote notebook
- A Microsoft Stream group
- A Microsoft Forms group
- These can be seen in the following diagram:

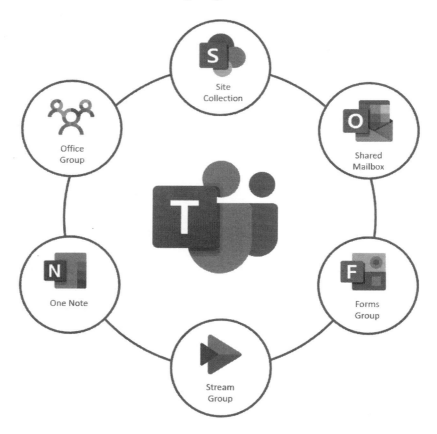

Figure 1.13: Microsoft Teams connected platforms

Adding members to the team

To add members to a team, do the following:

1. Select your team and click on the ... icon.

2. On the dropdown, click **Add Member**.

3. Start typing in the name or group you want to add.

4. While typing, you will get suggestions regarding users that belong to your organization. Find the user you want to add and click on them. If guest access is enabled on your tenant, you will be able to add members to the team that don't belong to the organization. To do this, type in the person's email and select **Add <email> as a guest**:

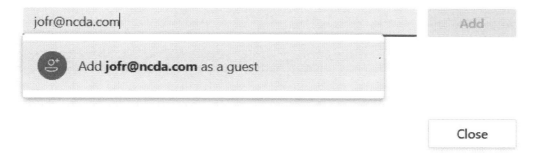

Figure 1.14: Add members to a team

5. Once the users have been added to the team, a post will be automatically made in the general channel to let everyone know about the new members.

Guest users are identified by the word (Guest) in front of their name and will not be displayed with a profile picture. To clearly identify a guest user, make sure they are added with a legible name. Microsoft Teams will suggest a name based on the email, but while adding the guest to the Team, you have the opportunity to rename them.

To change the name of a guest user, click on the pencil icon and type in a new name, as shown in the following screenshot. You might want to consider adding the organization of the user to their name in case you have users with the same name from different organizations:

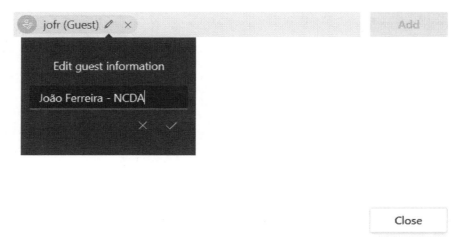

Add members to Woman's Basketball Team 19/20

Start typing a name, distribution list, or security group to add to your team. You can also add people outside your organization as guests by typing their email addresses.

jofr (Guest) ✎ ✕   Add

Edit guest information

João Ferreira - NCDA

✕   ✓

Close

Figure 1.15: Rename a guest user

So far you have learned how Microsoft Teams looks and how to create teams. In the following sections you will learn how to tailor your teams to your needs.

What is a channel?

A channel is a section inside of a team that helps you organize conversations, files, and tools inside a container.

By default, all teams are created with the General channel, which includes the conversations tab, files, and wiki.

Channels are public by default, but if it's been enabled by the administrator, it is also possible to create private channels. Private channels will be explained in detail in *Chapter 5, Public versus Private – Teams and Channels*.

Channel Scenario #1 – Mary the marketing manager

Mary is working with the company designers to create advertisements for a campaign. To avoid distracting other members of the team and to keep the information about this topic centralized, Mary has created a new channel. In the new channel, the team members working on the advertisements are doing the following:

- Chatting about the ideas to promote the campaign
- Sharing files, either specifications or the design files of the several concepts

Channel Scenario #2 – Geno the basketball coach

Geno has created his team ahead of the start of the season and is organizing a pre-season plan with his assistant coaches. Before adding the athletes to the team, Geno has created a Pre-Season channel so that he has/can do the following:
- Have a common place where the pre-season schedule can be shared.
- Communicate with the athletes and other staff member once the pre-season starts.

Creating a new channel

The creation of a new channel is straightforward and is always done in the context of the team where you want to create it. Therefore, to add a channel to the team, do the following:

1. Select the team and click on the ... icon.

2. Click on **Add Channel**.

3. Give a **name** to the channel, as well as an alternative description to help team members understand the topic or purpose of the channel.

4. Select if you want to automatically show the channel to the channel list of the team members:

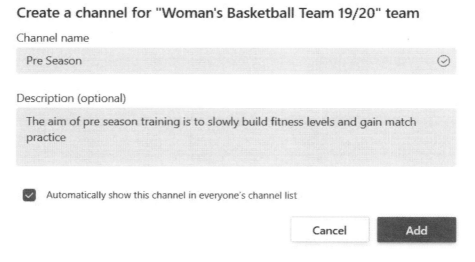

Figure 1.16: Create a channel

What happens when I create a channel?

When a public channel is created, it creates a folder in the document library of the team SharePoint site collection. Each new channel gets its own folder in the document library to keep files organized by topic.

Creating a channel also generates an email address that can be used to send messages directly to the conversations that are occurring on the team.

To get the email address for the channel, do the following:

1. Select the channel and click on the ... icon.

2. Click on **Get email address**. A popup will open and reveal the email address.

The use of email addresses can be restricted to avoid receiving unwanted messages in the chat window. To do this, from the **Get email address** popup, click on the **advanced settings** link and select one of the available options:

- **Anyone can send emails to this address**

- **Only members of this team**

- **Only emails sent from these domains:**

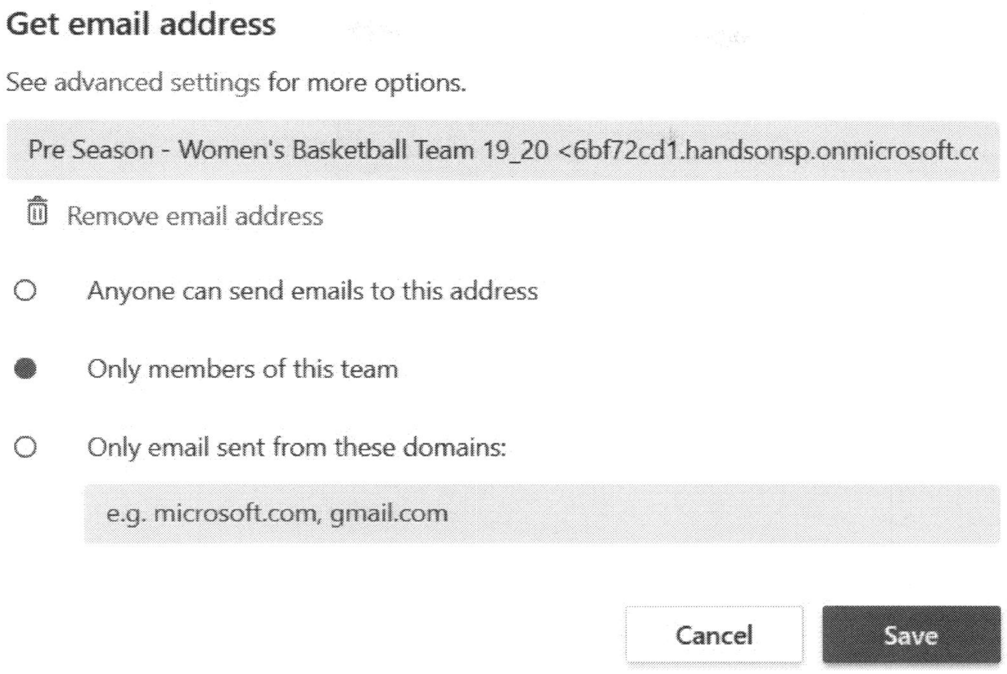

Get email address

See advanced settings for more options.

Pre Season - Women's Basketball Team 19_20 <6bf72cd1.handsonsp.onmicrosoft.co

🗑 Remove email address

○   Anyone can send emails to this address

●   Only members of this team

○   Only email sent from these domains:

e.g. microsoft.com, gmail.com

Cancel   Save

Figure 1.17: Manage email address settings

If you want to disable the email functionality of the channel, in the same popup, there is a link to remove it. Once the email has been removed, the option to get the email address will disappear from the dropdown.

In this section, you have learned how to create your own structure inside a team. In the following section , you will learn how to refine your structure even further using tabs.

What is a tab?

Tabs allow team members to access tools and content in the context of a channel inside a team. Tabs also allow team members to have conversations in the context of a tab to discuss the content the tab is displaying.

On Microsoft Teams, you will find two types of tabs: the built-in ones that come by default with the application and the custom ones that are added by apps that have been installed on Microsoft Teams, either from the store or manually uploaded.

> **Tab Scenario #1 – Mary the marketing manager**
> Mary wants to make sure the advertisements for the campaign are on track and to do this, she's added a new tab to the channel with Microsoft Planner, along with the tasks of each designer.

> **Tab Scenario #2 – Geno the basketball coach**
> Geno continues to prepare for the season. He wants to share the plays and the plan for his practice sessions with the players without printing everything out. Geno has added two tabs to the Pre-Season channel for the following reasons:
> •To add a OneNote document with all the plays and practice sessions.
> •To add a YouTube video showing the plays.

Creating a new tab

Tabs are created in the channel context. To add new tools to your channels, do the following:

1. Open the channel where you want to add a new tab.

2. On the stage section, next to the **Conversation and Files** tab, click on the + icon:

Figure 1.18: Create a new tab

3. From the **Add a tab** popup, select one of the available apps.

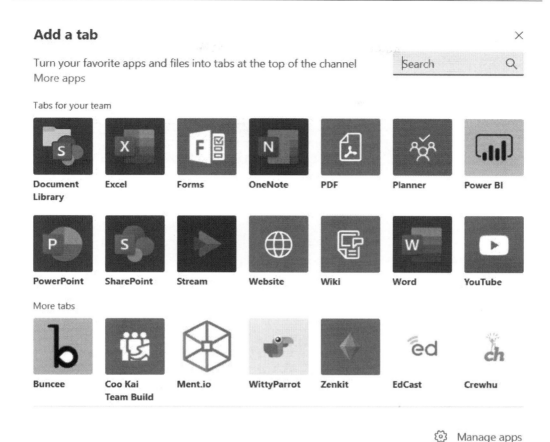

Figure 1.19: Select the app for the tab

4. If the app is not installed on Microsoft Teams yet, click on the **Add** button.

5. Configure the tab by following the options available in the form. Each app will present different options.

6. Click **Save**.

Using tabs, you will be able to create your custom structure inside of your channel. This flexibility allows you to adapt Microsoft Teams to virtually any scenario from any industry.

Summary

In this chapter, you learned about the basic concepts and operations of Microsoft Teams. Now, you are ready to start building your own teams. We can compare Microsoft Teams components to the Russian dolls with the Team, Channel, and Tab structure being the nested components inside of a team structure.

The three base concepts of Microsoft Teams are organized hierarchically and have dependencies between them. A tab can only exist inside of a channel and a channel can only exist inside of a team. This structure gives you the flexibility you need to build your teams by following the internal organization of companies or schools.

In the next chapter, you will learn how to use the main features of Microsoft Teams to communicate with other Teams members.

2
Microsoft Teams' Core Features

Now that you know what Microsoft Teams is and what it looks like, it's time to look at its core features and how you can use them to achieve more with the platform.

A hub for communication and collaboration, Microsoft Teams brings people together. It is Microsoft's carefully designed features that allow the platform to do this in such a unique way.

To get the best out of Microsoft Teams, you'll need to understand not only the basic concepts explained in the first chapter but also how to manage all of the assets that the platform brings together.

In this chapter, you will gain an overview of the following main topics:

- Understanding **chats** and **meetings**
- Managing your time using the Microsoft Teams calendar
- Working faster on Teams with **search**, **filters**, and **commands**
- Customizing Microsoft Teams
- Where is Microsoft Teams data stored?

Understanding chats and meetings

Microsoft Teams' main features can be divided into two major sections: **chat** and **meetings**.

The chat feature takes a principal role in Microsoft Teams and allows you to communicate with your peers in a few different ways, using text. You can have one-to-one or group chats, which can be public or private.

One-to-one chats are always private, and you will be able to start a new conversation with anyone from your own organization (an internal user) or from other organizations (a guest user).

Group chats, which you start manually by adding people to the chat, are private, while group chats that you start in the context of channels are public and accessible to all team members.

> **Note**
>
> The chat feature is heavily used by Microsoft Teams users and has many functionalities that deserve to be explained in detail. *Chapter 3, How to Use Microsoft Teams – Chats and Conversation,* is exclusively dedicated to chats and all of its built-in features.

The meetings feature on Microsoft Teams provides a rich environment to collaborate with peers who are not in the same location as you. It allows you to bring people from all over the world into the same room in a matter of seconds.

Meetings uses high definition audio and video and allows each member to share video and audio. It even allows screen sharing—you can share your entire desktop screen or individual application windows with other users.

Meetings on Microsoft Teams can also be recorded and shared with other members of the organization in a matter of minutes using Microsoft Stream. If you have a conflict in your schedule and are not able to attend the meeting, you can always watch the recording.

> **Note**
>
> *Chapter 4, How to Use Microsoft Teams – Meetings, and Live Events,* is exclusively dedicated to meetings, and you will find instructions there on how to use its built-in features.

Now that we understand what chat and meetings are, we still have to manage our meetings and schedule. Let's see how to do so in the next section.

Managing your time using the Microsoft Teams calendar

Microsoft Teams would not be a true collaboration solution if it were not equipped with a calendar. The calendar app is available by default on Microsoft Teams and allows you to view and schedule Teams meetings:

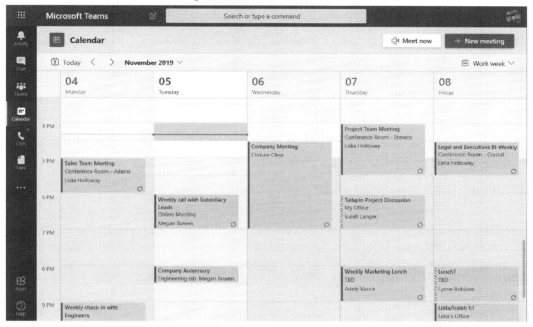

Figure 2.1: Microsoft Teams Calendar

The Microsoft Teams calendar includes the following features:

- Daily view.
- Weekly view: This view can display just the workdays or the entire week.
- The ability to view the meeting scheduling details.
- The ability to schedule a meeting or live event.
- The ability to cancel a meeting.
- Synchronization with Outlook and Exchange calendars.
- The ability to meet immediately, without previous scheduling.

> **Note**
>
> The detailed features relating to meetings and events are explained in *Chapter 4, How to Use Microsoft Teams – Meeting, and Live Events*.

In our next section, we will see how using different features will help make our work faster and enable us to save time when working on Teams.

Working faster on Teams with search, filters, and commands

All the collaboration work done using chats and meetings on Microsoft Teams will generate a considerable amount of data, which can easily reach hundreds of megabytes across all the teams and channels in an organization.

Microsoft Teams comes with three features that can help you find content and carry out tasks without spending hours looking for the information manually:

- **Search**
- **Filters**
- **Commands**

Let's look at each of these in more detail.

Search

The search feature is available in all versions of Microsoft Teams. On the desktop version, you can find it in the title bar right at the top of the application, as shown in the following screenshot:

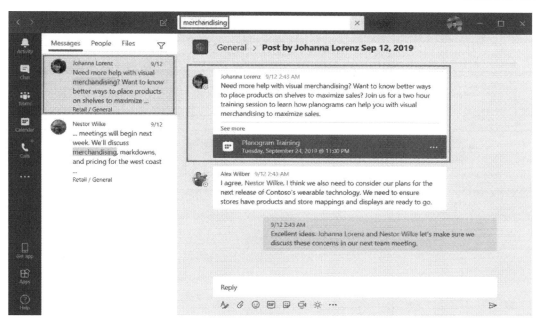

Figure 2.2: Microsoft Teams Search

The search feature looks for information in three different scopes:

- **Messages**
- **People**
- **Files**

The search results are displayed in the left pane and you can alternate between the scopes using the tabs at the top of the pane.

When you click on one of the results displayed in the **Messages** tab, it opens the message in the context it was sent, that is, in the team, channel, or one-to-one chat where the message is located.

If you are looking for a team member and click on one of the results shown in the **People** tab, you will get access to a private chat window with that particular member.

The results shown in the **Files** tab are displayed in their Microsoft Teams context. For example, a Microsoft Word document will be opened in the web version of Microsoft Word in the stage area. If the file is not compatible with the Microsoft Teams preview functionality, you will have the option to download the file locally or open it in a browser.

The mobile version of Microsoft Teams has the same search functionalities available as the desktop version, and the search feature is also located at the top of the app. To use it, you will need to click on the magnifier icon and type in your search query. The results are then displayed in a separate window divided into the same three categories: **Messages**, **People**, and **Files**.

Filters

The filters function offers another way to find content inside Microsoft Teams. You can use this feature, along with search, to filter the results retrieved or you can use it in the context of **Activity**, **Chat**, and **Teams**.

To use filters to refine your search results, you will need to click on the filter icon next to the tabs on the left pane, as in the following screenshot.

Once you have clicked on the filter icon, a popup will appear that will allow you to filter all the metadata associated with the results retrieved:

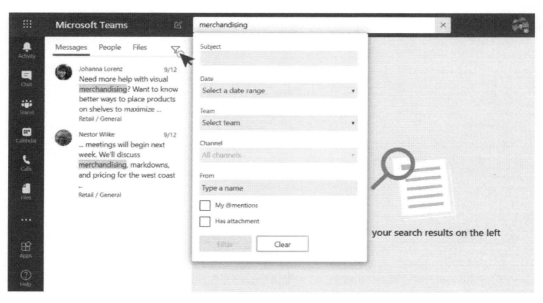

Figure 2.3: Filter search results

This popup is dynamic and displays different fields depending on the context of your search. In the context of the search function, it is only available for **Messages** and **Files** and it is not possible to filter **People**.

Outside of the search context, the filter option also has its own search box and predefined tags that you can select in order to get to the information faster.

To filter in the context of **Activity**, **Chat**, or **Teams**, click on the filter icon and type what you are looking for in the textbox. To use the predefined tags, click on the three dots (…) and choose one of the available options. The tag feature is only available in the **Activity** and **Chat** contexts:

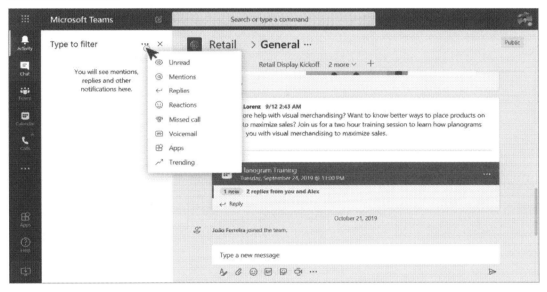

Figure 2.4: Chat tags

Once a tag is selected, a word is added to the text box, immediately filtering the results, and can be combined with your own search query to refine the results even further.

Unlike the search feature, filters are only available in the desktop versions of Microsoft Teams. You will not be able to use this feature in the mobile app.

Commands

Commands are designed to make you work faster on Microsoft Teams. They are shortcuts for tasks such as opening a channel or changing your availability status. There are two types of commands—the ones built into the Teams application and the ones added by third-party apps.

To use the built-in commands, you will need to type / into the command box at the top of the screen, followed by the command you want to use.

Commands will perform simple tasks. Some of them will trigger the command action when you type them, while others will require data from you to trigger the action. The following screenshots show two different examples of things you can do in Microsoft Teams using commands.

If you type /busy, your presence status will be modified to busy:

Figure 2.5: Presence set to busy

If you type /chat, the search bar will change the layout and you will have access to your contacts list and a textbox to send a message. This is particularly handy if you are in a meeting and need to send a private message to someone:

Figure 2.6: Sending a quick chat to a Microsoft Teams user

The following table from the official Microsoft documentation lists all of the available commands. This list might change in the future as new functionalities are added to the platform. To view all of the available commands at any given time, you can type / in the search bar:

Command	Description
/activity	See someone's activity.
/available	Set your status to available.
/away	Set your status to away.
/busy	Set your status to busy.
/brb	Set your status to be right back.
/call	Call a phone number or Teams contact.
/chat	Send a quick message to a person.
/dnd	Set your status to do not disturb.
/files	See your recent files.
/goto	Go right to a team or channel.
/help	Get help with Teams.
/join	Join a team.
/keys	See keyboard shortcuts.
/mentions	See all your @mentions.
/org	See someone's org chart.
/saved	See your saved messages.
/testcall	Check your call quality.
/unread	See all your unread activity.
/whatsnew	See what is new in Teams.

Some apps can install command functionalities. These are also available from the search bar. To use them, you will need to type @ followed by the name of the command. Typically, these types of commands are used to bring information from outside the organization into Teams.

For example, if the Microsoft weather app is installed in your Microsoft Teams tenant, you will be able to get the current weather for any city when you type the @Weather command followed by the name of the city:

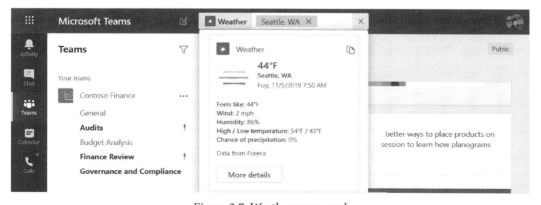

Figure 2.7: Weather command

Both built-in and third-party commands are only available on the desktop version of Microsoft Teams. This feature is not available for mobile clients.

In this section you learned how to get things done more quickly using Microsoft Teams shortcuts. Knowing how to use the command bar effectively will improve your productivity while working with Microsoft Teams.

Customizing Microsoft Teams

Even though Microsoft Teams is a working platform, it allows you to customize certain features and settings to make it fit better with your working preferences and routines.

To access the configuration settings of Microsoft Teams, do the following:

1. On the Microsoft Teams client, click on your profile picture and then click on **Settings**:

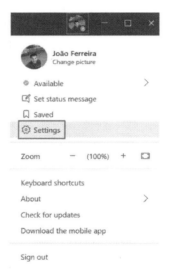

Figure 2.8: Personal settings

2. A popup will open, and from there you will have access to six different groups of settings:

   (a) **General**: In this group, you will be able to access the Microsoft Teams themes. The default is a light theme, but a dark and a contrast theme are also available. From the **General** tab, you can also select the language for the app and keyboard, as well as general application settings, such as autostarting the application and using Teams as the default chat app for Office:

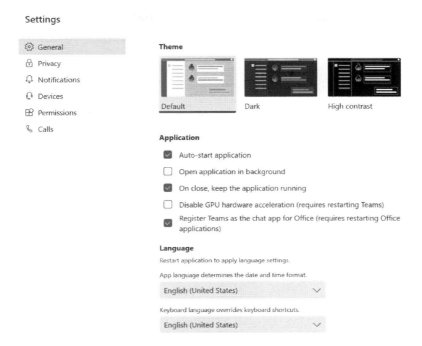

Figure 2.9: General settings

(b) **Privacy**: In the privacy settings, you will find an important option that allows you to prioritize notifications from certain people when your status is set to **Do not disturb**:

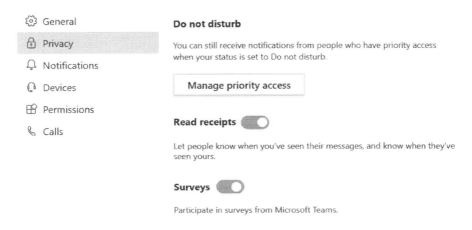

Figure 2.10: Personal privacy

Here, you can also decide whether other users can access your read receipts on the app. A read receipt is displayed next to a message, with an icon representing an eye, and tells other people that you have read their messages:

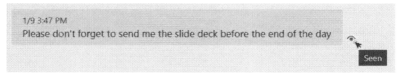

Figure 2.11: Read receipts

(c) **Notifications**: Notifications on Microsoft Teams will help you to prioritize what is most relevant to you. Your notifications can be personalized with four different options. You can choose whether a notification is displayed in the banner, in the banner and over email, only in the feed, or off completely. However, these options are not available for all notifications, and some cannot be turned off. In the following screenshot, you can see all of the notifications that can be customized in Microsoft Teams:

Figure 2.12: Notifications

At the bottom of the **Notifications** page, you will find a **Manage notifications** button. This option allows you to select individual contacts and be notified every time they are online or offline.

(d) **Devices**: This option allows you to select which devices will be used for audio and video on Microsoft Teams. Here, you also have the option of making a test call to make sure everything is working as expected. When attending a meeting or a live event, you can always override the settings defined here and use other hardware available on your device:

Settings

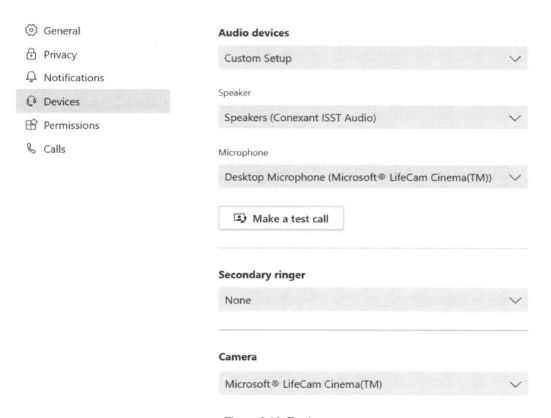

Figure 2.13: Devices

Once you have selected the devices you want to use, Microsoft Teams offers you the possibility of testing them on a test call. To perform a test call, you need to click the **Make a test call** button.

(e) **Permissions**: To get the most out of all of Microsoft Team's features, the application has consent to use several things from your device, such as the location or the physical hardware for meetings and live events. If you want to revoke access to the peripherals or to settings such as **Location**, you can do so in this tab:

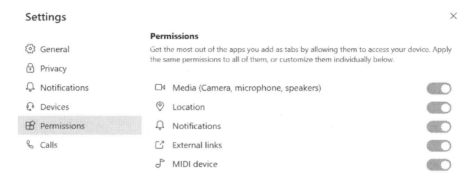

Figure 2.14: Permissions

(f) **Calls**: In this tab, you will find everything related to the calling features on Microsoft Teams. You can configure the voicemail options and the ringtone when someone calls you:

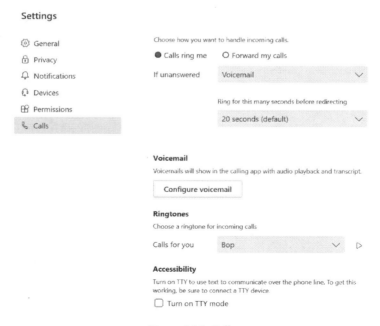

Figure 2.15: Calls

Microsoft Teams gives you the option to manage your settings individually and this section covered each one of the options individually. Once you start using Teams, make sure you have a look at each one of these sections to ensure that Teams is adjusted to your needs and preferences.

Now that we have an overview of what Microsoft Teams' core features are and how to use them, you might be curious to know where all that data is stored. Let's look at this in more detail in the next section.

Where is Microsoft Teams data stored?

Microsoft Teams makes use of several Office 365 services to deliver features to a central location. It is important to know that your data is not stored in a central location, as it may appear when using the Teams applications and, depending on the feature, your data might be stored in different locations.

Microsoft Teams' data is stored in all of the following apps. Some data is available to you through the app, while other information is hidden and only displayed in the Microsoft Teams client:

- **Microsoft Exchange**

    (a) One-to-one chats are stored in your mailbox in a hidden folder that is not available to other users. This data can only be viewed through Microsoft Teams. (The hidden folder is available through the information protection tools if needed for legal reasons.)

    (b) Voicemails are stored on the user mailbox and the data is available in Microsoft Teams.

- **Microsoft Stream**

    (a) Meeting recordings are stored on Microsoft Stream. Users can access the recordings on the Stream portal.

- **SharePoint**

    (a) Files shared in channels are stored on the team site collection. Each channel has a folder in the documents library on SharePoint. Users can access the files from SharePoint or Microsoft Teams.

- **OneDrive for Business**

    (a) Files shared in one-to-one chats remain on the OneDrive of the person who shared it and permissions are given automatically. Microsoft Teams does not copy files to the user's OneDrive when shared in one-to-one chats. Users can access the files from OneDrive (files are located in the Microsoft Teams **Chat Files** folder) or from Microsoft Teams.

The following diagram is a graphical representation of where Microsoft Teams stores files and which apps are used to do so:

Figure 2.16: Microsoft Teams features and used platforms

Summary

This chapter provided an introduction to the main features included in Microsoft Teams and gave you an overview of how they work and what they look like. In the upcoming chapters, you will see that these features are common across the Microsoft Teams apps, making it really intuitive.

Chats and **meetings** are key features of Microsoft Teams. They are complemented by other features, such as **file sharing**, **search**, and **calendar**, which allow you to be more efficient as you carry out your daily tasks.

In the next chapter, we will cover the chat feature in Microsoft Teams in more detail.

3
How to Use Microsoft Teams – Chats and Conversation

Communication is the key to success when working in a team. Microsoft Teams allows you to leverage your communication skills with little effort by providing a set of tools that allow you to chat with your peers in a matter of seconds.

The chat features included in the product allow you to have private and public written conversations and help you to keep everything organized and centralized for easy access.

In this chapter, we are going to cover the following main topics:

- Understanding the chat feature on Microsoft Teams
- How to use private chats
- How to manage contacts

- How to use the chat application
- Understanding the message options
- Understanding chats in the context of teams

Understanding the chat feature on Microsoft Teams

Chat is a default application found in the app bar and allows you to start a written conversation with any member of your organization.

Before jumping into your first conversation, it is best to understand how the chat app is organized to get the most out of it. The following screenshot shows a page in the app, with its main components highlighted and described:

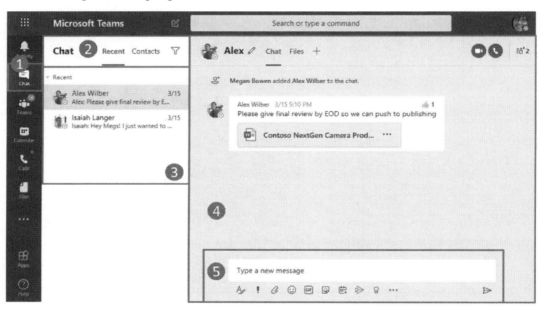

Figure 3.1: Chat layout

Let's cover each of these components in detail:

1. **The Chat app**: The **Chat** application gives you access to the private chat feature on Microsoft Teams.

2. **The Contacts tab**: The contacts tab allow you to find other Microsoft Teams members to start a conversation.

    (a) **Recent**: This shows you the latest contacts you chatted with and also suggests contacts based on your recent activity. The **Recent** tab also displays your pinned contacts; these contacts are always displayed at the top for faster access.

    (b) **Contacts**: This list is built by you and it will show all of your favorite contacts.

3. **Your chat contacts**: A list of contacts, filtered by the selected tab.

4. **A chat thread**: This is where you can access a chat thread and where you will see all the assets shared during a conversation. It is also the place where you can access other Teams apps using the tabs at the top of the section.

5. **The chat box**: This is your input element for the conversation. From it, you can write text and upload files, as well as carry out other functions, which we will look at later in this chapter.

Throughout this chapter, we will look at the Chat elements in more detail.

How to use private chats

Private chats can be used to have conversations about topics that are not relevant to an entire team. You can use it to plan your daily tasks with your co-workers or even to schedule a coffee break. All of the content shared in private chats will only be visible to you and the other members of the chat.

Microsoft Teams supports one-to-one and one-to-n private chats (with a limit of 100 users). In this section, we will look at how to use both.

To start a new one-to-one private conversation using Microsoft Teams, follow these steps:

1. Click on the **Chat** app in the app bar.

2. Look for the user in the left pane that you want to chat with and click on their name.

3. Start your conversation.

Even though this three-step process is the easiest way to start a chat on Microsoft Teams, sometimes the user you want to chat with will not be available in the contacts list. In this case, do the following:

1. In the top bar of Microsoft Teams, click on the **New chat** icon, seen in the following screenshot.

2. In the stage area, type the name of the person you want to chat with. In the left pane, you will see that a new chat has been created.

3. Click on **New chat** and start your conversation. The chat thread will be added to the **Recent** section in the left pane:

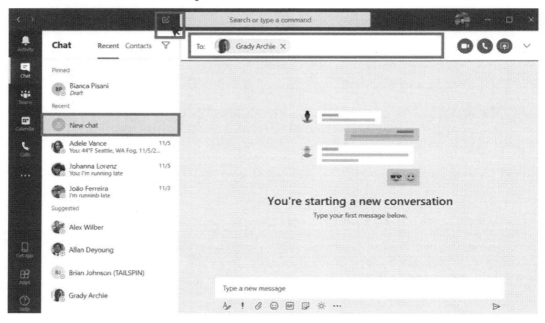

Figure 3.2: New chat

Microsoft Teams also supports private group chats outside the scope of a team. To create a new group chat, follow these steps:

1. In the top bar of Microsoft Teams, click on the **New chat** icon, seen in the following screenshot.

2. Click on the arrow on the right side of the stage area.

3. Provide a name for the group; this helps you to identify your group chats.

4. Add members to the group chat.

5. Click on the chat box and start your group conversation. As with one-to-one chats, group chats will also appear in the **Recent** section in the left pane:

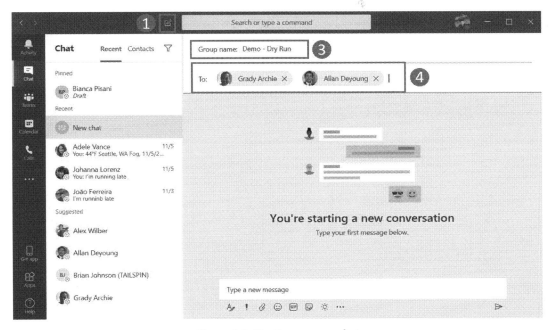

Figure 3.3: Starting a group chat

Over time, you might need to include someone else in a private group chat. This could cause privacy issues, especially if you have messages in the chat that were not supposed to be read by any new members.

To avoid having to create a new private group chat, you can take advantage of the chat history feature, which allows you to control how much of the chat history the new member can access:

- None of the chat history
- *X* days of the chat history
- All of the chat history

This option appears at the top of the chat window whenever you add additional members to the chat, as the following screenshot shows:

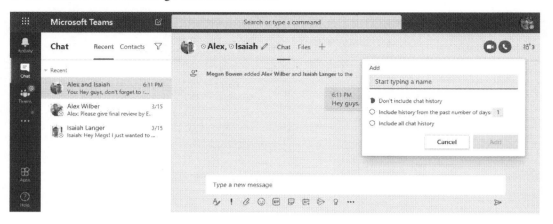

Figure 3.4: Privacy settings when adding a new member to the chat

How to manage contacts

You will not chat with all members of your organization in the same way and you will likely have a set of contacts that you will use more frequently and want to access quickly.

To create your own list of personal contacts, do the following:

1. Open the **Chat** app.

2. In the **Recent** tab in the left pane, hover over the contact you want to add to your personal list.

3. Click on the three dots (…) to open the context menu of the contact.

4. Click on **Add to favorite contacts**.

Your favorite contacts will be listed in the **Contacts** tab in the left pane, organized in alphabetical order:

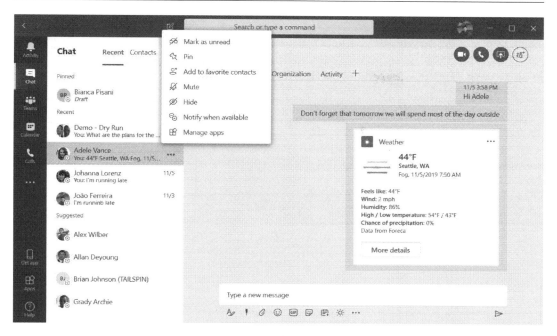

Figure 3.5: Chat options

The context menu for each contact gives you access to more features and actions that you can use to carry out your work more effectively:

- **Mark as unread**: If you accidentally click on a chat when there are new messages available to read but you simply don't have time to read them, this option allows you to mark the chat as unread so you don't forget that there are new messages that need your attention.

- **Pin**: If you want a contact to always be visible in the **Recent** tab, you can use this option. It is particularly handy in scenarios where you don't want to miss any updates from a user and want to reply quickly. A pinned contact is displayed in the first group of the **Recent** tab and you can pin up to 15 contacts.

- **Mute**: If you need to focus but you have colleagues always pinging you, this option allows you to mute them. A muted contact will not trigger any notifications on Microsoft Teams.

- **Hide**: If you know you won't be speaking to one of your colleagues any time soon, you can use this option to remove the contact from the **Recent** tab. This way, you will only be focusing on the conversations that matter.

- **Notify when available**: This option triggers a notification every time a user becomes available on Microsoft Teams, so you can start a conversation immediately. This option is only available to users that belong to the same organization.

Now that we are familiar with the application and how to set it up, in our next section we will see how to use the chat app and its different features.

How to use the chat application

The chat app on Microsoft Teams comes equipped with functionalities that go beyond writing text. To send a message inside the chat app, do the following:

1. Click on the text box in the chat thread.

2. Type your message.

3. To send it, press *Enter* or click on the send button.

At this stage, everything looks like a regular chat app, such as the ones we have on our phones. However, things start to get interesting when you use the extra functionalities provided by Microsoft Teams. In the following image, you can see the text box with a set of icons underneath. Each icon allows you to enrich your messages:

Figure 3.6: Text box

> **Bonus tip:**
> If you post a message and, right after pressing *Enter*, notice that something is wrong and needs to be fixed, press the **up arrow** on your keyboard. When you do this, the **edit text box** opens inside the thread and you can fix your mistake using all of the options provided by the chat box. Modified messages are tagged with a label '**Edited**' indicating that the message was edited by the author.

Let's now see what each of these icons are and how to use them, starting with the default features of Microsoft Teams.

Format

The **Format** option provides a rich text editor that allows you to format your texts to add greater clarity to your messages. The toolbar offers options to format fonts and styles, similar to the ones you find on Microsoft Word. There are also options to build lists, add quotes, tables, or even snippets of source code, with the options of selecting a programming language. As with any text editor tool, while composing your message you have the option of undoing or repeating your typing:

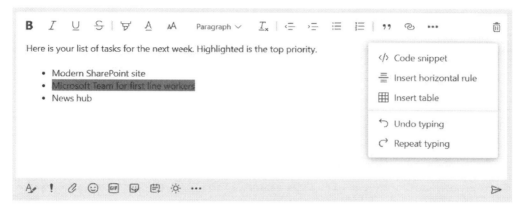

Figure 3.7: Text box with formatting options

Set Delivery Options

Not all messages have the same priority. In Microsoft Teams, you can clearly identify a message that needs attention as soon as possible by using the delivery options:

- **Standard**: This is the default option on Microsoft Teams. A message is added to the chat and a notification is sent to the user you are chatting with.

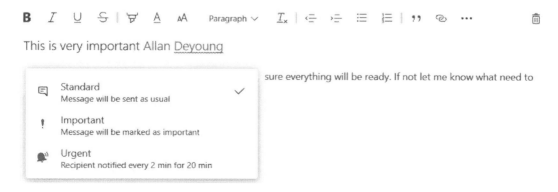

Figure 3.8: Standard message

- **Important**: The message is marked with an **IMPORTANT!** tag in the chat thread. The user that you are chatting with will be able to identify it by its red color and the! icon in the message box:

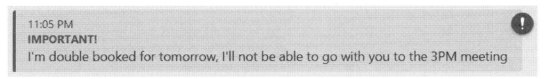

Figure 3.9: Important message

- **Urgent**: The message is marked with an **URGENT!** tag in the chat thread. The user you are chatting with will be able to identify it by its red color and by the bell icon in the message. A notification is sent to the user every 2 minutes for a duration of 20 minutes:

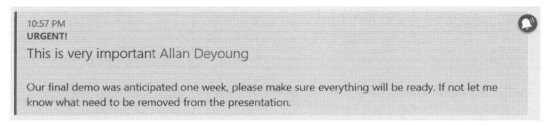

Figure 3.10: Urgent message

Attach

Attach allows you to add files to a message. Files can be uploaded from your computer or your OneDrive account. The files attached from OneDrive display the path where the file is located and the ones uploaded from your computer only display the name of the file, as shown here:

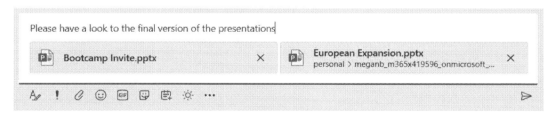

Figure 3.11: Message with attachments

Files attached to a chat thread are available in the thread itself or in the **Files** tab at the top of the **Chat** app, as in the following screenshot. The files attached from your computer to a chat are copied to your OneDrive into a folder with the name **Microsoft Teams Chat Files**. Permissions are automatically assigned, so other users in the conversation can also access the files. The **Files** tab provides you with a central view of all the files shared in a chat, so you don't have to scroll through an entire conversation thread to locate them:

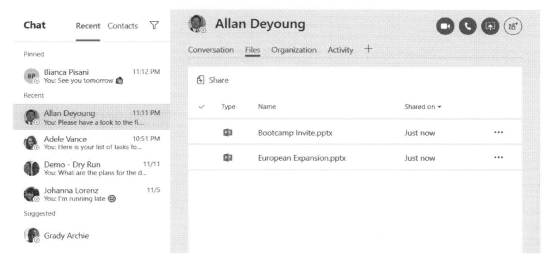

Figure 3.12: Files shared in a conversation

Bonus tip:

Images can be added inline with the text instead of as an attachment. To add an inline image, copy the image to the clipboard and then paste it when you are composing the message. The images added inline with the text will only exist in the thread and will not be copied to the OneDrive folder. If you want a copy of the image to be accessible in the OneDrive folder and the **Files** tab, you will have to attach it to the message.

Emojis

Emojis allow you to express emotions in your messages. The emoji box includes a search box, which will help you to locate the emoji you are looking for to use in the message. It also shows you the shortcut command for the emoji when you hover your mouse over the image for longer than 2 seconds, as in the following screenshot:

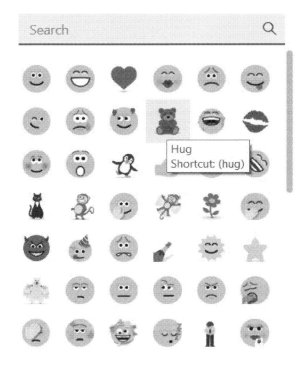

Figure 3.13: Emojis

Emojis on Microsoft Teams are animated and can be displayed in two different sizes. When added alongside text in a message, they are displayed as the same size as the text. When sent as an individual message, they are displayed in a bigger size, as shown here:

Figure 3.14: Emojis with different sizes

Modern operating systems have hundreds of hidden emojis for you to use. To access this *Easter egg* feature on Windows 10, press the *Windows key* + . and a new emoji menu will open, as in the following screenshot. On macOS, press *command* + *control* + the *spacebar*.

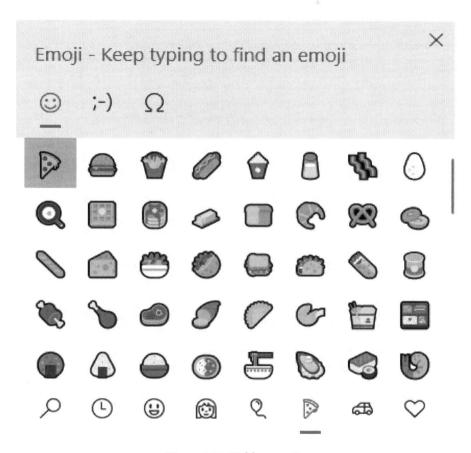

Figure 3.15: Hidden emojis

Giphy

Giphy can also be used to express emotions in your messages or to react to another user's message. Even though this is a default option on Microsoft Teams, the GIFs are provided by an external service.

Stickers

Stickers just like emojis and GIFs, allow you to react to messages. Stickers are static images that have an option for customization. Once you have selected the image you want to send, you are given the option to write your own message, as in the following screenshot:

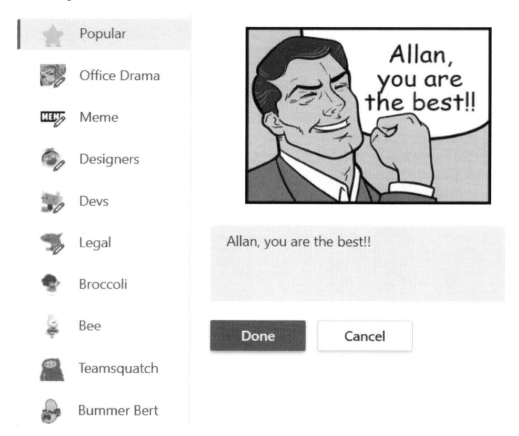

Figure 3.16: Stickers

Schedule a Meeting

Schedule a meeting allows you to immediately schedule a meeting with the person you are chatting with without going into the calendar. The meeting is scheduled using all the options that are available in the calendar app. Once scheduled, the meeting is not added to the chat but instead goes directly into the calendar app:

New meeting ⌄

| Title | | Select a channel to meet in |
| | | None (optional) ⌄ |

| Location ⌄ | Invite people |
| | Invite someone |

Start		End		Repeat ☐	Organizer
Nov 16, 2019	9:00 AM	Nov 16, 2019	9:30 AM		👤 João Ferreira
					JoaoF@M365x419596.OnMicrosoft.c...

Free: No suggestions found   🕐 Scheduling assistant

Time Zone	Attendees
(UTC+00:00) GMT Standard Time ⌄	👤 Allan Deyoung ✕
	Unknown

Details

B *I* U̲ S̶ ᴥ̶ A AA   Paragraph ⌄ T̲ₓ | ⇐ ⇒ •••

Close   **Schedule**

Figure 3.17: New meeting

Messaging Extensions

Messaging extensions is the last option available in a chat using Microsoft Teams with the default configuration. This option allows you to configure the chat box even further by adding on extra functionalities. It also allows you to use other apps that, despite already being installed, are not displayed in the toolbar. **Praise** and **Stream** are two examples of apps that are available by default but hidden in this menu:

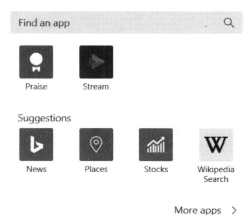

Figure 3.18: Messaging extensions

Praise: Sometimes, you want to tell a member of your team how valuable they are to the organization, but you can't find the right words. This app helps you to do so by allowing you to select the type of praise you think your team member deserves. You can also type a message along with your chosen praise. This makes it easier to recognize the value of your peers. The praise is added to the chat window with a badge displayed inside an adaptive card:

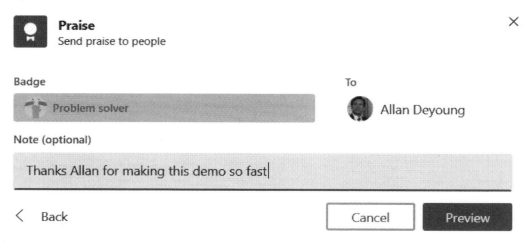

Figure 3.19: Praises

Stream: Stream allows you to embed a video from Microsoft Stream directly into your conversation. All you need to do is copy the URL of the video and paste it into the app window. The video is added to the chat window inside an adaptive card and, before posting it, you can add a message to personalize the card. Writing a message is handy if you want to describe the content of the video and useful if you want to later locate it through the search feature:

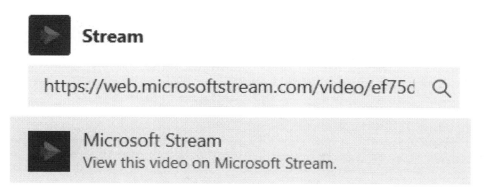

Figure 3.20: Microsoft Stream

In Microsoft Teams, you will find more apps that can enrich the functionalities of your chat. To add more options to your chat box, do the following:

1. Click on the **…** icon.

2. From the popup, select the app you want to add or click on **More apps**.

3. Type or look for the app you want to add (for example, **Weather**).

4. Click on the app you want.

5. The app details will pop up on the side. Click on **Add**:

Figure 3.21: Add weather messaging extension

6. The app will be added to the toolbar with its own icon, as in the following screenshot:

Figure 3.22: Weather messaging extension

When you click on the newly installed app, a popup will open and allow you to select the content (for example, the **Weather** app provides you with a search box to look for the location where you want to share the weather). The content from the app is then added to the chat thread inside an adaptive card.

Understanding message options

Each message posted in the chat app has a set of options available that you can use to manage, react to, or categorize each message. To access the message options, you will need to do the following:

1. Hover your mouse over the message, wait for the three dots (...) to appear, and then click on it.

2. A contextual menu will appear, as in the following screenshot, and you will be able to select a message option:

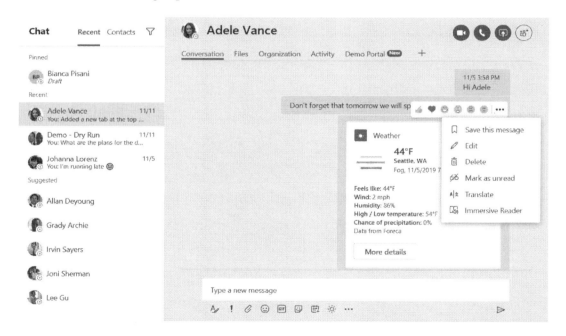

Figure 3.23: Message options

The contextual menu will be different for messages sent by you than for the one displayed on messages you receive. The available options are detailed in the following sections.

Saving Messages

Save this message allows you to save a message to your **Saved** list. A messaged that is saved by you is marked with a bookmark icon and is added to the **Saved** list, which means you will be able to later locate it faster from a central location.

To access your saved messages, do the following:

1. Click on your profile picture at the top of the Microsoft Teams client.

2. From the profile contextual menu, click on **Saved**.

3. Your saved messages will all appear in the left-side pane with a preview of each message. When you select a message, it opens up in the conversation where it happened:

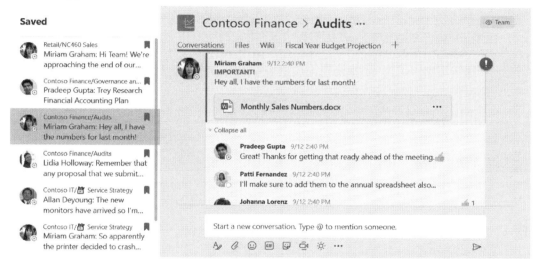

Figure 3.24: Saved messages

Editing Messages

Edit is only available for the messages you send, and it allows you to modify the contents of a sent message. Each edited message is marked with a tag to let other users know that the original text was modified.

Deleting Messages

Delete is only available to you and it allows you to remove a message from a chat thread. However, it only deletes the contents of the message; the message itself will remain in the same chat position with a replacement message saying **This message has been deleted**.

Mark as Unread

Mark as unread allows you to mark messages as unread. This is handy if you need to go back to a particular message. It will be highlighted in **Teams** as unread.

Translate

Translate translates messages from different languages to your own automatically. As you can see in the following screenshot, the original message was written in Portuguese and then translated to English. Translated messages will display a language icon and, when hovered over, will show a popup telling you what the original language was:

Figure 3.25: Message translation

Immersive Reader

Immersive Reader will open up Microsoft Teams in read mode, where you will only see text, as the following screenshot shows. This option does not allow you to interact with a message. To reply or react to it, you will need to go back to regular mode. If you click on the play button, it will read the message back to you:

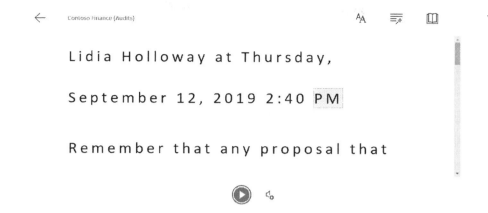

Figure 3.26: Immersive reader

Besides being a great tool for accessibility, **Immersive Reader** also includes educational features, such as highlighting the nouns, adjectives, or verbs in a text.

Reacting to Messages

You can also react to each message you have received or sent using emojis. To use this feature, do the following:

1. Hover your mouse over the message until the context menu appears. Emojis will appear at the top right on the message.
2. Select your desired emoji.

There are six reactions available in the messages, as follows:

- Like
- Heart
- Laugh
- Surprised
- Sad
- Angry

Each message will display how many users have selected a particular emoji. The sender of the message is notified every time someone reacts to it:

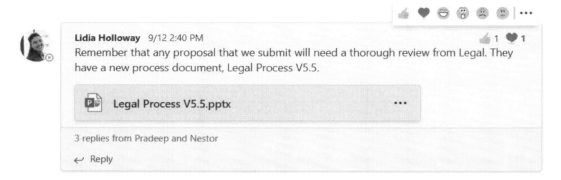

Figure 3.27: Message reaction

Up to now in the chapter, we have seen the different features of the chat app and how to use them. However, chats are a bit different when used in teams, which is what we will cover in the next section.

Understanding Chats in the context of teams

Chats in the context of a team have the same functionalities as described previously. However, due to the different scope of the conversation, there are also a few other options available that will help you to communicate better and be more productive.

The chat feature is the first tab in the channel. It is called **Posts** and its position and label cannot be modified.

Each channel inside of a team starts with its own chat app, which allows you to have conversations with all of the members of a team, relating to the topic of the channel. The following section describes the special features that this app has.

Reply versus typing a new message

Unlike individual chats, where everything is displayed as an individual message, in a channel, things can quickly get out of control if everybody uses the **new message** feature.

In a channel post, each message will display a **Reply** button underneath. This is the option you should use to reply to the message.

Once you click on **Reply**, a chat text box will appear at the bottom of the screen, containing all of the options that we previously discussed, as in the following screenshot:

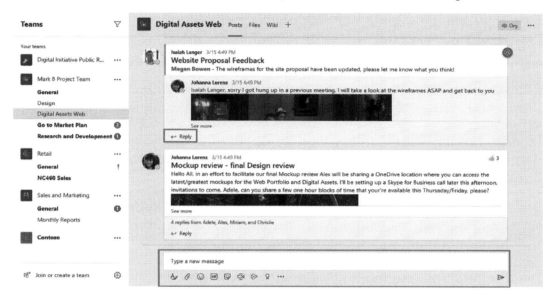

Figure 3.28: Reply versus new conversation

You should always reply to conversations using the **Reply** button under the message, as this way you can keep conversations organized and easier to read.

Replies made outside of the thread will lose their order and, if multiple topics are being discussed in the same channel, it will become impossible to follow the conversation.

Keep in mind that each time you start a new conversation, instead of creating a reply, your message is added to the bottom of the chat as a new conversation. In the following screenshot, the last message should have been a reply to the thread and, as you can see, it has no connection to the original conversation:

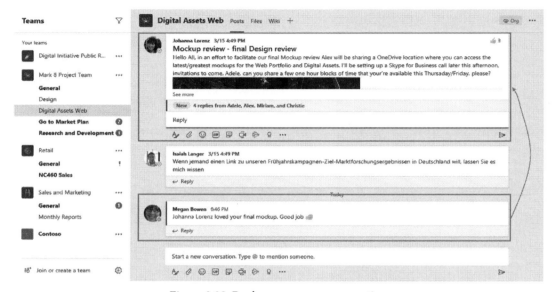

Figure 3.29: Reply versus new conversation

Making an announcement

Chats in the context of a team allow you to post announcements. Announcements are messages that allow more customization and that can be more easily identified by a user in the chat thread.

To create a new announcement, do the following:

1. In a team channel, click on the chat text box and then click on the first icon to expand the **compose** box.

2. Open the **New conversation** dropdown and choose **Announcement**:

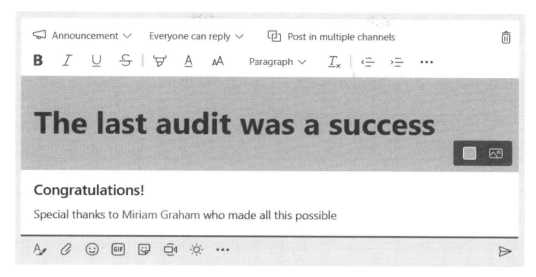

Figure 3.30: Writing an announcement

3. Type a headline for the announcement.

4. Select a background color or background image.

5. Type a sub-headline.

6. Type your message and click on the send button.

An announcement will display a special icon on the right side and has a different format in the chat thread to give it a more distinctive look, as you can see in the following screenshot:

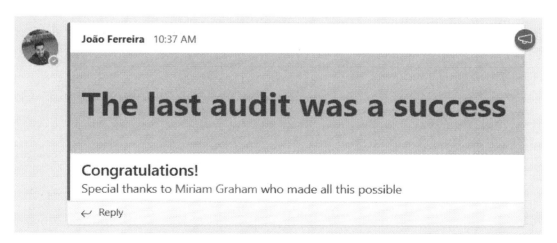

Figure 3.31 Announcement in the chat thread

Targeting a post's replies

When posting a message in a channel, you can define who will be able to reply to it. By default, all team members are able to reply, but you can restrict this scope by doing the following:

1. In a team channel, click on the chat text box and then click on the first icon to expand the compose box.

2. From the second dropdown, choose the audience that will be able to reply to the message. By default, everyone can reply, but you can modify it to **You and moderators can reply**:

Figure 3.32: Target post reply

Posting in multiple channels

If you need to post the same message over and over again in multiple channels, to make sure it reaches everyone, you can use the following option to help simplify the process.

To post a message in multiple channels, do the following:

1. In a team channel, click on the chat text box and then click on the first icon to expand the compose box.

2. Click on the third option in the toolbar: **Post in multiple channels**.

3. Select the channels that you want to post your message to:

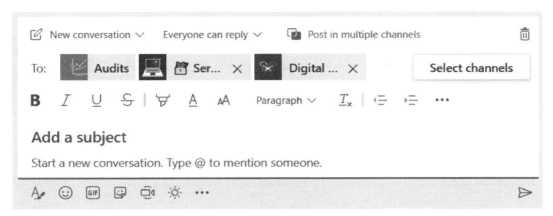

Figure 3.33: Post in multiple channels

4. Type your message and send it.

A message posted in multiple channels is identified by a special icon in the chat thread to tell you that it exists in multiple locations.

If you need to monitor the replies to this message, you will need to do so in each channel that the message was posted in, as this information is not shown in a central location.

Muting a thread

If you are receiving a lot of notifications from a channel that you're not currently interested in, there is an option to mute that particular thread. To use this option, do the following:

1. Hover your mouse over the main message in the thread you want to mute.

2. Click on ... to open the context menu.

3. From the context menu, select **Turn off notifications**, as in the following screenshot:

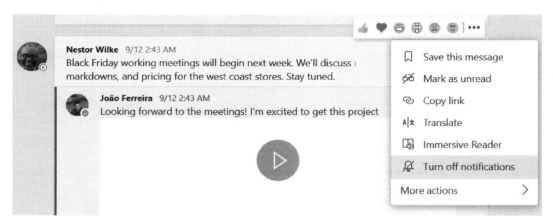

Figure 3.34: Turn off notifications

Mentioning a user, team, or channel

Microsoft Teams allows you to mention colleagues inside a team or a group chat. When typing your message, you will need to do the following:

1. Type @ followed by the name of the user, team, or channel that you want to mention.

2. From the suggestion list, select the user:

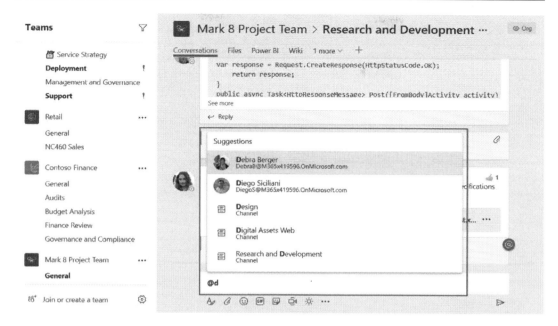

Figure 3.35: Mention a user

When you are mentioned in a chat, the message is marked with an @ symbol, so you can easily spot it while reading the thread, as in the following screenshot:

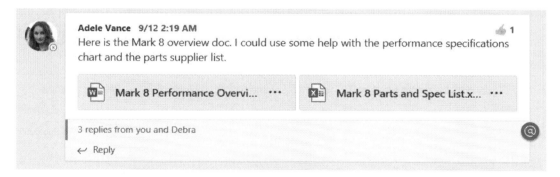

Figure 3.36: Message indicating the user was mentioned

When a team is mentioned, everyone in the team receives a notification. When a channel is mentioned, everyone that has the channel marked as a favorite will receive a notification.

Using tags

Tags in Microsoft Teams allow you to message groups of users within a team. Tags can be added to users by the team owners or members (if allowed by the team owner in the team's settings).

To add tags to users on Microsoft Teams, do the following:

1. Next to the name of the team, click on **…** and then click on **Manage team**:

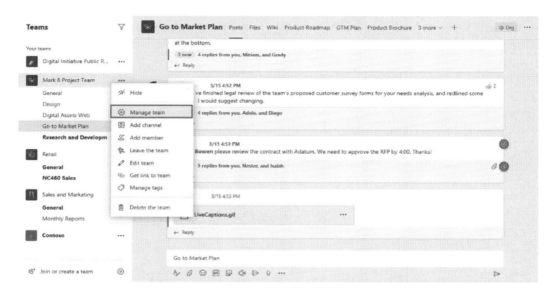

Figure 3.37: The Manage team menu option

2. Open the **Members** tab.
3. Hover your mouse over the field in the **Tags** column for the member that you want to add a tag to and click on the tag icon:

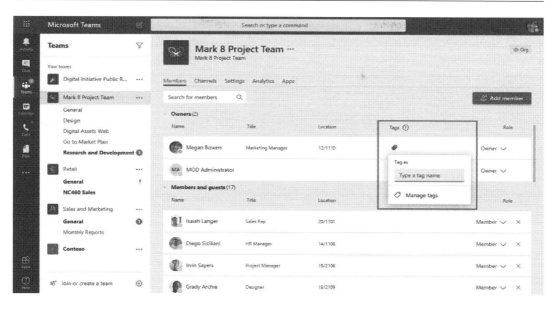

Figure 3.38: Tagging a user

4. If you have tags that are already created, type the name of the tag. If you want to add a new tag, click on **Manage tag**.

5. In the popup, click on **Create tag**.

6. Type in a name for the tag and add the users that you want to add to the tag:

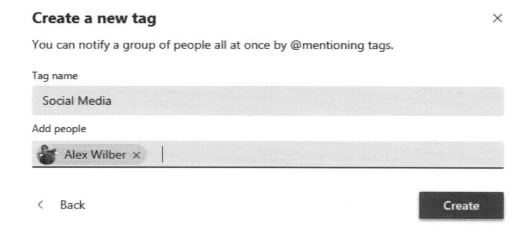

Figure 3.39: Create a new tag

7. Click on **Create**.

If, later on, you want to add an existing tag to another user, you just need to click on the tag icon in the list of users and, from the dropdown, select the desired tag, as in the following screenshot:

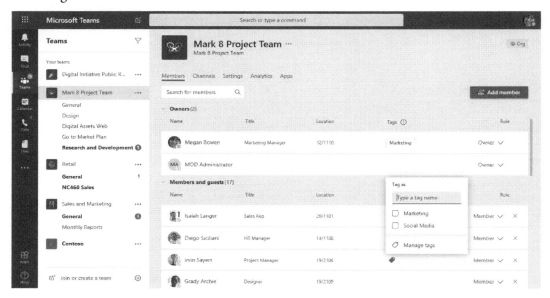

Figure 3.40: Tagging a user

To mention all of the users tagged in the same topic, you only need to press the @ key and select the name of the tag:

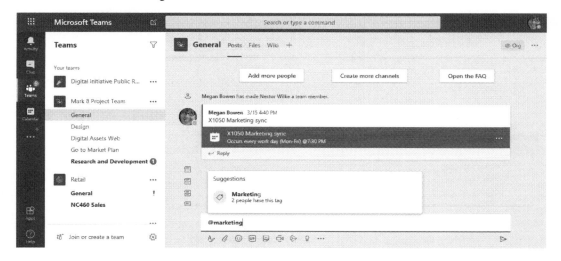

Figure 3.41: Mentioning a tag

Starting a new channel conversation from Outlook

Each channel in Microsoft Teams has its own email address, which can be used to start a new conversation in the channel. An email sent to the channel will include the body of the email and any attachments. However, if you plan on using this feature, you should be aware of the following limits:

- The maximum message size: 24 KB

- The maximum number of attachments: 20, less than 10 MB each

- The maximum number of inline images: 50

If these limits are exceeded, the message in Teams will display a link to open the original message.

To obtain a channel's email address, do the following:

1. Go to the channel you want to email.

2. Click on **...** and then **Get email address**:

Figure 3.42: Get email address

3. Copy the email address that appears in the popup.

4. Send an email from your email client. The message should appear in the channel as follows:

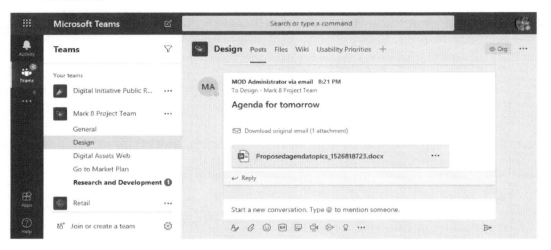

Figure 3.43: Message sent by email

In this section, you gained an overview of all the major chat features included in Microsoft Teams. Keep what you have learned in this chapter in mind while using Teams to make sure you follow best practices as you do so.

Summary

In this chapter, you have learned how to use Microsoft Teams to chat with your peers in multiple contexts.

A written message can be much more than a simple piece of text. This chapter has demonstrated how we can use Microsoft Teams to communicate better and improve efficiency when carrying out daily tasks.

In the next chapter, you will learn how to use Microsoft Teams' calling functionality and about other tools that you can use to complement everything you have learned so far.

4
How to Use Microsoft Teams – Meetings and Live Events

The evolution of the different web technologies and the increment of speed in terms of network connections is changing the way we all consume information and the way we all work.

The web is no longer a place where you can only find written content; more and more people are looking for video content since it is easier to consume and understand what is being explained.

This chapter covers the media functionalities of Microsoft Teams in terms of meetings and live events and explains all the main features. This will help you to decide when to use each of them.

In this chapter, we are going to cover the following main topics:

- How to schedule a meeting

- Available options during a meeting

- How to schedule a live event

- What are live event profiles?

- Available options during a live event

Meetings in Microsoft Teams

As a substitute for Skype for Business, Microsoft Teams has a lot of calling and meeting functionalities that extend communication to a new level in a modern workplace.

A meeting in Microsoft Teams can start spontaneously by just clicking on a button. It can also be planned ahead of time and scheduled by generating a meeting request that can be sent to other participants.

In the following section, you will learn how to schedule a meeting and how to use all the options to get the best out of the media functionalities of Microsoft Teams.

How to schedule a Microsoft Teams meeting

Meetings can be scheduled directly from the Microsoft Teams application or from the desktop version of Microsoft Outlook if the Teams add-on has been installed on your computer and allowed by your administrator.

To schedule a meeting from Microsoft Teams, do the following:

1. Open the **Calendar**. The app is available in the App Bar.

2. Click on the purple icon that says **New meeting**:

Figure 4.1: New meeting

3. On the form, fill in the following details for your meeting:

(a) **Title**: The title of the meeting.

(b) **Location**: The location for the meeting. You will be able to pick a meeting room or type a location in.

(c) **Start**: Start time.

(d) **End**: End time.

(e) **Repeat**: Make this a recurrent event. If you select this option, you will have the possibility to define the meeting's recurrence.

(f) **Time Zone**: In a multi-geo workplace, it is important to define the time zone. Users who are invited to the meeting in other time zones will see the time converted into their own location's time automatically.

(g) **Details**: This field is ideal for providing information about the meeting so that anyone can prepare for it before joining.

(h) **Channel**: Select the team and the channel where the meeting will occur.

(i) **Attendees**: Add attendees to the meeting:

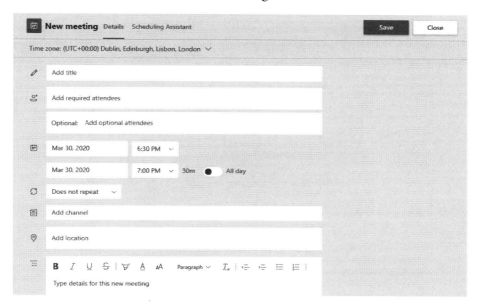

Figure 4.2: Scheduling form

4. Before scheduling the meeting, you can use the scheduling assistant to avoid meeting overlaps. If everything is OK, click on **Schedule**.

Alternatively, you can start a meeting spontaneously without scheduling it. To do so, you just need to click on the **Meet now** button in the Calendar app, and once the meeting has started, you will be able to add other participants.

Meetings can also be scheduled or started from a team context. If you want to have a meeting with all the members of a team or want to discuss a subject that is being handled by the team, it makes sense to schedule it directly from the team. This will create the meeting and keep all the meeting assets centralized in the team space, making it easier to access the information.

To schedule a meeting directly from a team, do the following:

1. Open the team and the channel where you want to have a meeting.

2. Click on the **Meet now** option located in the text bar:

Figure 4.3: Meeting from the channel

3. A configuration pane will expand, as shown in the following screenshot. Here, you will have the option to add a subject to the meeting and to **Meet now** or **Schedule a meeting**. If you choose to schedule a meeting, a popup will open with the same options we saw when we scheduled a meeting from the Calendar app:

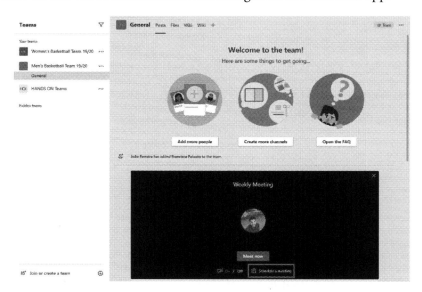

Figure 4.4: Scheduling a meeting from the channel

4. If you select **Meet now**, you will have the option to invite members from the team once the meeting has started. Each invited member will receive a notification on the app to join the meeting.

If you are replying to emails or checking your calendar in Outlook and have the need to schedule a meeting, there is an add-in that allows you to send out the meeting request without the need to switch to the Microsoft Teams context.

To schedule a meeting from Microsoft Outlook, do the following:

1. On Microsoft Outlook, open the Calendar app.

2. On the top bar, click on **New Teams Meeting**, as highlighted in the following screenshot:

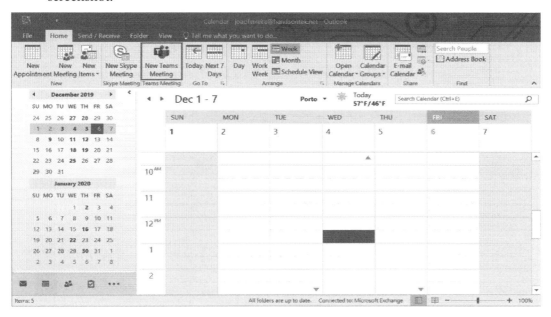

Figure 4.5: Scheduling a meeting from Outlook

3. Type in the emails of the users you want invite to the meeting.

4. Type in the subject.

5. Select the location.

6. Select the date.

7. Personalize the meeting request if needed and click **Send**.

> **Note**
> Scheduling a meeting from Outlook doesn't give you the option to select a channel.

Each user that's added to the meeting request will receive an email with the link for the meeting. Users will be able to join the meeting either by clicking on the link in the meeting request or by clicking on the meeting in the Calendar app on Microsoft Teams.

How to customize Microsoft Teams meeting requests

Branding is one the most important aspects in the enterprise world. A company logo tells a lot about a business, and Microsoft Teams has taken this into consideration.

Teams allow us to customize meeting requests in such way that every time you invite someone external to the organization, they can be easily identified if we look at the logo of their organization or company. Also, by adding the company logo, you are creating brand awareness.

To customize the meeting requests for your organization, do the following:

> **Note**
> The following steps are only available for Microsoft Teams administrators.

1. Open **Microsoft Teams admin center**. You can do this by opening the Microsoft 365 Admin Center and then choosing **Teams** or by simply opening the following URL: https://admin.teams.microsoft.com

2. On the left panel, select **Meetings** and then **Meeting Settings**.

3. In the **Email invitation** section, you have the option to customize four fields related to your meeting requests:

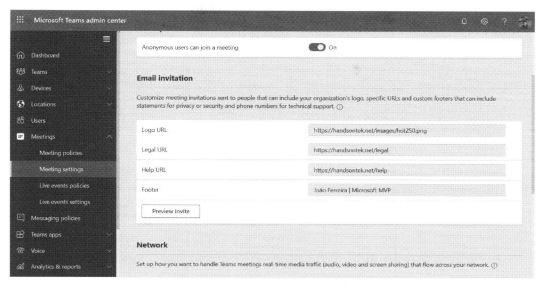

Figure 4.6: Email customization form

These four fields are as follows:

(a) **Logo URL**: The URL where the logo is stored. You will need to publicly host the logo yourself. The logo format must be JPG with the dimensions 188 x 30 pixels.

(b) **Help URL**: Use this to add a URL where people can get help if something doesn't work as expected with the meeting.

(c) **Legal URL**: If your organization has a legal website where you want people to go to if they have legal concerns, enter the URL in this field.

(d) **Footer**: Small text that is displayed at the bottom of your meeting request.

4.   Click on **Preview invite** to make sure it looks as you expect:

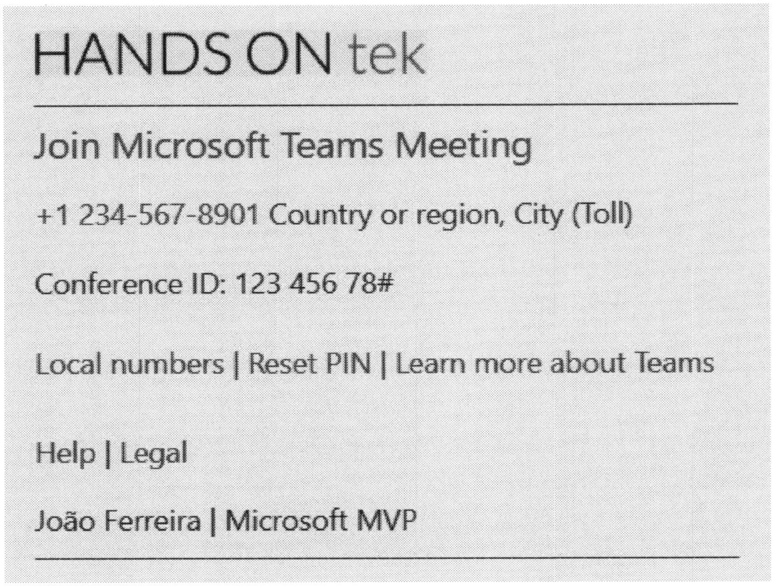

HANDS ON tek

Join Microsoft Teams Meeting

+1 234-567-8901 Country or region, City (Toll)

Conference ID: 123 456 78#

Local numbers | Reset PIN | Learn more about Teams

Help | Legal

João Ferreira | Microsoft MVP

Figure 4.7: Customized meeting request

5.   If everything is OK, scroll to the bottom of the page and click **Save**.

The customization options will not be available immediately. You will have to wait about an hour to see that it has been added to new meeting requests. This customization will be added to all meeting requests, irrespective of the place where they were created.

What are the available options during a meeting?

Now that you know how to schedule a meeting, it is time to learn more about the meeting interface and the available options you will find. The following screenshot shows all the main meeting components, numbered from 1 to 7.

Before joining the meeting, you will have the option to set up the devices that you will use to interact with the other participants; namely, your webcam, microphone, or other audio and video devices you may have in your environment:

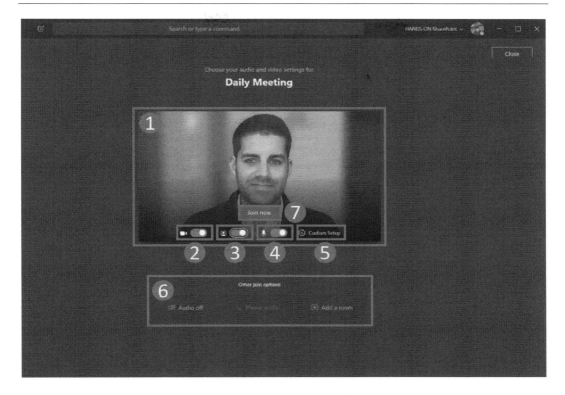

Figure 4.8: Meeting setup options

Let's take a look at the available components and what they do:

1. **Video preview**: In this area, you will be able to preview how the image of your webcam will look to the other participants.

2. **Webcam toggle**: Video is not mandatory during a Microsoft Teams meeting but if you have a webcam, I recommend that you use it. By default, it is turned on, but this option allows you to turn it off.

3. **Blur background**: This option is only available when the webcam is on and if supported by the hardware of your computer. It adds a blur effect to the background, focusing just on the person in the video. Alternatively, you can select a background image that will replace your entire background. This is particularly handy if you want to hide the elements in the room or open workspace where you are having the meeting. We will see more on this later on in this chapter.

4. **Microphone toggle**: Like the webcam, the microphone is not mandatory if you are joining a meeting just to listen. Make sure you turn off the mic. By default, it is on. Microsoft Teams automatically turns off the mic if four participants are already in the meeting. This behavior can be overwritten and you can turn it back on.

5. **Device settings**: This option allows you to select the devices you want to use during the call. If you have multiple speakers, microphones, or webcams connected to your computer, you will be able to select the ones you want to use in this menu. From here, you will also be able to perform a test call to make sure everything is configured properly so that you can join the call and interact with the other participants without any issues. This option might have different names; it may show your device name or it may say **Custom Setup** if you have customized the hardware to use:

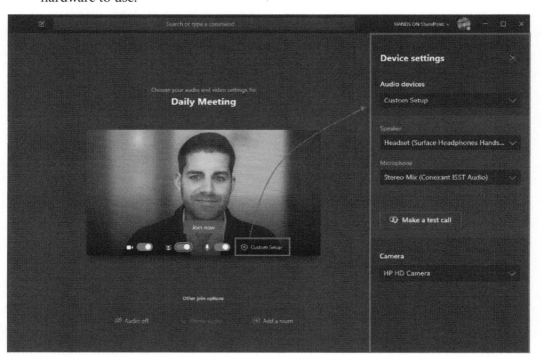

Figure 4.9: Meeting custom setup

6. **Other join options**: There are a few other options you can configure when joining a meeting that are available in this bottom section:

    (a) **Audio off**: This option prevents echo if there is already a device with a microphone turned on in the room.

    (b)**Phone audio**: If the organizer of the meeting has a Microsoft 365 Audio Conferencing license, you will be able to join the call using a phone number.

    (c) **Add a room**: If you are in a Microsoft Teams room with certified devices for Microsoft Teams, you can add them to the meeting using this option. Typically, rooms are added using Bluetooth, so make sure you have it on your computer. A room usually includes a big screen, a wide camera, and ambient microphones so that everyone can participate without using their own devices/computers.

7. **Join now**: Once you have your environment prepared for the meeting, click on this button to join.

Meeting options

Now that you know how to prepare your own device to join a meeting, it is time to learn what the available options are once you are in the call.

During meetings, participants can assume two different roles:

- **Presenter**: A presenter has the option to share content, take control of a presentation or control the microphones of all participants, remove people from the meeting, or accept participants from the lobby.

- **Attendee**: An attendee is not able to share content. The attendee is able to interact with other members but will not be able to manage any of the meeting settings.

With these two profiles in mind, let's see what the interface looks like to them, depending of the actions they are taking during the meeting.

The following screenshot represents the view for presenters and attendees. It has all the main meeting options highlighted:

Figure 4.10: Meeting layout with options

Let's take a look at these options:

1. **Personal meeting controls**: This toolbar allows you to control the meeting at a personal level and displays the options according to the user profile during the meeting.

2. **Bottom pane**: This section can assume different behaviors, depending on what is being shared in the meeting. If someone is presenting, you will be able to see the attendees at a glance by the order in which they have joined the meeting. If no one is presenting during the meeting, you will be able to see your webcam image if you have it turned on. You will also be able to switch between webcams if the device you are using has more than one installed. The switch camera button appears at the top of your image as an overlay.

3. **Presenting area**: This section also assumes different behaviors if someone is presenting the content being displayed in this section; otherwise, it is used to display the images of the participants, regardless of whether they are using a webcam. The following screenshot displays the different behaviors assumed by the bottom pane and by the presenting area:

Figure 4.11: Meeting layout without content being presented

4. **Right pane**: The right pane is used to display all the participants or to allow people to participate in the written conversation during the meeting.

> **Bonus tip**
> When you join a meeting, Microsoft Teams changes its theme and displays everything in black. This is a visual way for you to identify that a meeting is occurring.

Personal meeting controls

The personal meeting controls are worth a closer look, and the following section explains all the available options and actions you can take from it. Each option is highlighted and, when necessary, is identified in terms of which profile it is available from:

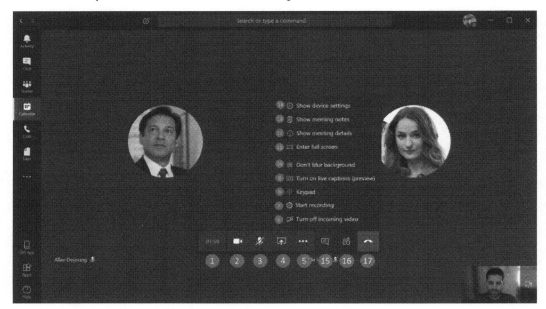

Figure 4.12: Personal meeting controls

Let's take a look at these options:

1. **Meeting duration**: This counter indicates the duration of the meeting. When hovered over, it displays the name of the meeting.

2. **Camera switch**: You can turn the webcam on or off at any time during a meeting using this option.

3. **Microphone switch**: Like the camera, the microphone can be turned on or off whenever you want during a meeting. This option is particularly handy if you need to have side conversations during a meeting. This way, your background noise will not disrupt the other participants.

4. **Share**: This allows you to share content in the presenting area with all the other participants. You can share your screen, applications, or even documents. This option is not available to attendees; only presenters have the option to share content in the meeting. You can find more information about the sharing features in the next section, *Sharing content during a meeting*.

5. **More actions**: This option gives you access to more personal options that allow you to control extra meeting options. These extra options are displayed in a submenu that opens when the user clicks on this button. These options are explained in the following points, from numbers 6 to 14:

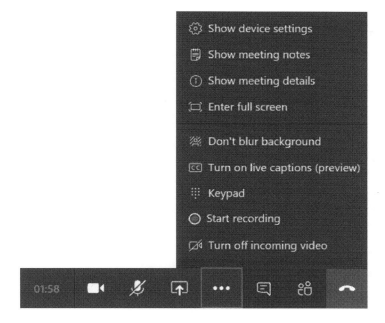

Figure 4.13: More actions menu

6. **Incoming video switch**: This option turns off any incoming video from other participants. It comes in handy when you have the need to free bandwidth on your network connection.

7. **Recording**: This option allows you to record a video of the meeting. Everything shared by any participant will be on the final video. You can find more information about the meeting recordings in the *Managing meeting recordings* section.

8. **Keypad**: During a meeting, if you have a need to dial a number, you can do so from this numeric keypad.

9. **Live captions**: Live captions translate anything that is being said by the other participants. Live captions appear at the bottom of the presenting area.

10. **Background blur switch**: Using video during a meeting is always a plus, but sometimes, the place where you are is not ideal or you simply don't want to share what is behind you. The blur option gives you the possibility to blur the background to hide everything except the person. In the following screenshot, you can see what it looks like with this option on and off:

Figure 4.14: Background blur

As an alternative, and instead of bluring the background, you can select one of the availabe photos in the application that will replace your entire backgroud. The option to select the blur option or the image becomes available when you toggle the blur switch:

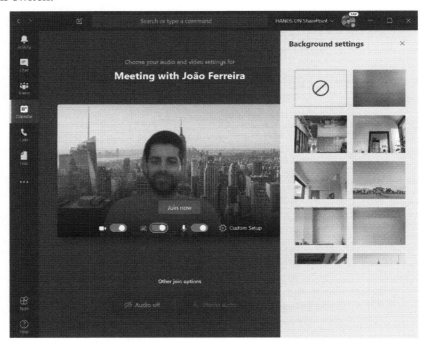

Figure 4.15: Background image

11. **Enter full screen**: This option maximizes the content of your call and removes all the window bars and menus, leaving just the call options.

12. **Show meeting details**: The meeting details option provides information related to the meeting, such as the subject, schedule, dial-in options, and also the possibility to copy the link to join to the clipboard.

13. **Show meeting notes**: This option is very handy and allows you to take notes during the meeting. The notes are stored in the meeting context and can be visualized by any participant at any given time. The notes option appears on the right pane and when they are created, a message is posted in the chat to let the other participants know that notes were created. To find out more about the meeting notes, read the *Managing meeting notes* section.

14. **Show device settings**: If you have the need to modify the device settings during a meeting, you can use this option. From the right pane, you will be able to manage microphone and camera settings.

15. **Show conversation**: This option makes the conversation visible on the right pane. From here, you will be able to interact using text with the other participants.

16. **Show participants**: From this option, you will be able to see all the participants in a list format. If you are a presenter, you will have extra options, namely, the possibility to promote an attendee to presenter, to make a presenter an attendee, or to mute participants. You will also be able to add or remove participants.

17. **Hang up**: This option will disconnect you from the call.

Sharing content during a meeting

Sharing content during a call is one of the best options when using the meeting functionality on Microsoft Teams. It can be used to present a PowerPoint Presentation , to share a screen, or even to perform remote assistance using the remote control functionality.

To share content during a meeting, you must be a presenter. Attendees do not have the possibility to share. As a presenter, in order to share content with other participants during a meeting:

Click on the share button (marked as **1** in the following screenshot) in the meeting toolbar.

A menu will appear at the bottom of the screen, where you will have the option to select what content you want to share, as shown in the following screenshot:

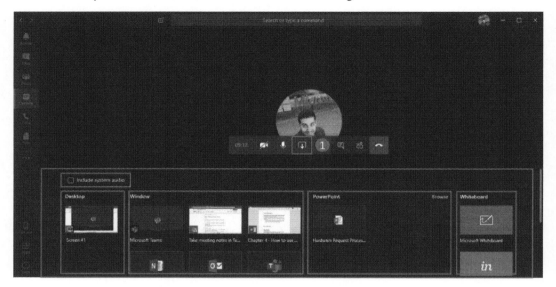

Figure 4.16: Sharing content

This functionality gives you the possibility to share content from different sources, such as the following:

- **Include system audio**: Optionally, you can include your system audio by checking this box.

- **Desktop**: Shares everything you are seeing on your desktop with the other participants. While sharing your desktop, a red rectangle is added to your screen to tell you the content is being shared.

  When a desktop is being shared, there is an option to request remote control. If you are in a meeting and want to request remote control over the presenter desktop, you will need to click the button highlighted in the following screenshot:

Figure 4.17: Request control button

The presenter needs to accept the remote control request by clicking **Allow** in the message that appears at the top of the stage area:

Figure 4.18: Requesting control message

- **Window**: If you do not want to share everything, you have the option to select just one window. This allows you to open other widows without sharing its content. When you open another window as a presenter, the other participants in the call will continue to see the window you shared initially, even though it's covered by other windows in your screen.

- **PowerPoint**: If you have a PowerPoint presentation to share during the meeting, you can do so directly from Microsoft Teams without opening the PowerPoint application. PowerPoint files can be shared from three different locations, as shown in the following screenshot:

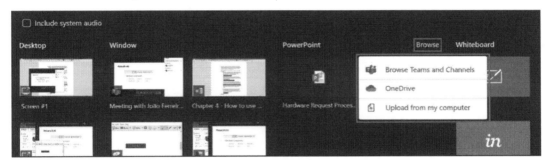

Figure 4.19: Sharing PowerPoint

(a) **Browse Teams and Channels** : This option allows you to select a PowerPoint file that is stored in one of the teams or channels that you have access to.

(b) **OneDrive**: If the PowerPoint Presentation is not stored in the Teams context but it is on your personal OneDrive, you can select it using this option.

(c) **Upload from my computer**: If the presentation is local to your computer, you can upload it to be shared using this option.

By default, all meeting participants are able to interact with the PowerPoint Presentation being shared:

(a) **Presenters** are able to take control and change the PowerPoint slides. The following screenshot displays the presentation controls for all the second presenters. The PowerPoint controllers are only displayed when the user hovers over the presentation:

Figure 4.20: PowerPoint controls

As a main presenter, you can block the option for others to change the slides. The following screenshot displays the controls for the main presenter. The option to block slide interaction from other attendees is highlighted and is represented by an eye icon:

Figure 4.21: PowerPoint presenter controls

This option does not block the possibility for other presenters to take control. Every time someone takes presentation control, the main presenter is notified by a message displayed at the top of the presenting area, with the possibly for them to take control back again:

Figure 4.22: Taking presentation control back

At any given time during the presentation, you can also take control back by clicking the take back control button in the presentation controls.

(b) **Attendees** are able to change the slides if the presenter hasn't blocked that feature. The following screenshot displays the default controls for attendees. When the presenter locks the option to change the slide, an attendee will only see the number of the slide without the navigation arrows.

Figure 4.23: Limited presentation controls

• **Whiteboard**: Whiteboard allows you to take handwritten notes or draw during a meeting while everyone is watching it. The following screenshot displays the Whiteboard application with some handwritten content on it:

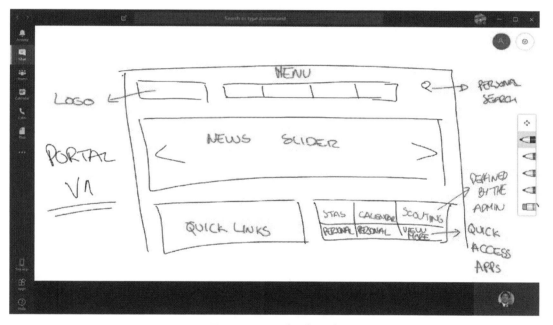

Figure 4.24: Whiteboard

To get the best out of the sharing features of Microsoft Teams, it is recommended that you use the client version, even though Google Chrome and Edge Chromium are able to support the sharing functionality. If you use the browser, you will lose the option to share individual windows.

Managing meeting recordings

All the meetings you have on Microsoft Teams, with or without sharing content, have the possibility to be recorded. When a recording starts, all the participants are notified and a red icon is displayed next to the meeting clock to inform everyone that the meeting is being recorded, as shown in the following screenshot:

Figure 4.25: Meeting bar with the recording information

The participants are notified with a recording disclaimer, as shown in the following screenshot:

Figure 4.26: Recording notification

Even when the meeting is done only using audio, the recording is done in a video format and is hosted right after the meeting in a cloud service called Microsoft Stream.

Note that all meeting recordings are made in the cloud and the person that starts it doesn't need to remain in the meeting.

The meeting recording can be found in the meeting chat or in Microsoft Stream. To get the meeting recording from the Teams context, do the following:

1. Click on **Chat**.

2. In the recent list, select the meeting you want to get a record of.

3. Look for it in the **Chat** section. It will look similar to what is displayed in the following screenshot:

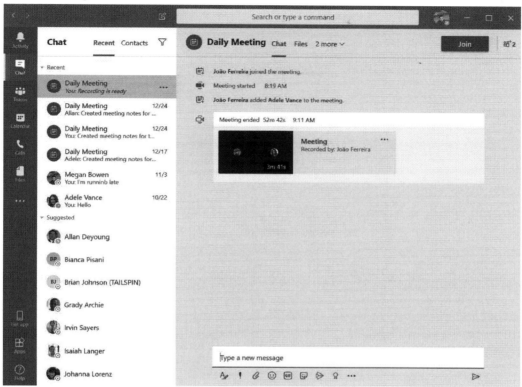

Figure 4.27: Recording post

4. To watch the recording, you just need to click on the video thumbnail and a popup will open with it.

To access the meeting recordings using Microsoft Stream, you need to do the following:

1. Open Microsoft Stream in the browser.
2. On the menu, click on **My content** and then **Meetings**.

3. All the meetings that you have recorded or that have been shared with you will be visible in this section, as shown in the following screenshot:

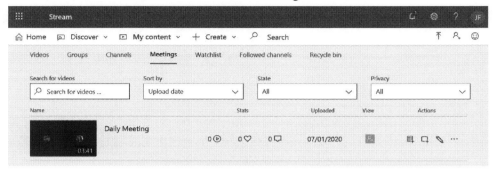

Figure 4.28: Recording on Microsoft Stream

Once the record is available, you will have access to a set of actions that will help you share the video with colleagues who were not able to attend the meeting.

To provide the best experience to people watching the recording, it is recommended that you edit the settings of the video and the metadata. To do so, you will need to click on the pencil icon under the **Actions** section. From there, you will get access to four main groups of options that you can use to make sure the recording reflects exactly what you want and that everyone watching it gets the right message. Let's take a look at what these four options are:

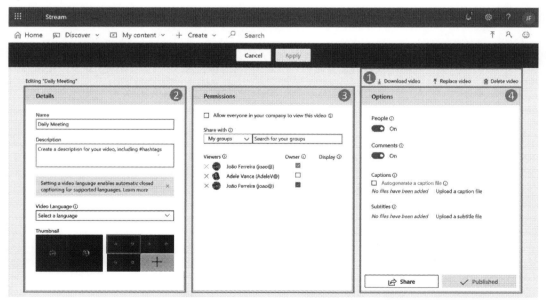

Figure 4.29: Managing a recording with Microsoft Stream

The following is an explanation of these options:

1. **Main actions**: In this section, you will be able to download the video locally to your computer, delete it for all the users if the recording is no longer relevant, or replace the video with another video file. The replace option is handy, especially when something went wrong with the original recording. This way, you will be able to replace it and people will be able to access the meeting content after it has occurred.

2. **Details**: By default, the details section only has the name filled in, and it inherits the name of the meeting. In this section, you are able to modify the name, add a description, and select the video language. The video language is a useful setting. Once it has been defined, it will generate a caption file automatically, making your video easy to find.

3. **Permissions**: By default, all the meeting participants inside your organization will have access to the video, but if you want to have fine control, you can by sharing it globally or restricting access to a certain group of people.

> **Note**
>
> Participants who are external to the organization will not have access to the video recording, even though it becomes visible in the meeting chat. This is caused by a current limitation of Microsoft Stream that only works with accounts that belong to the same organization. As a workaround, to share a video with external members, you can download the mp4 video file of the recording and store it inside a Team document library where external users have access.

4. **Options**: This section allows you to enhance the experience of the video. The **People** option creates a timeline showing who is presenting the video. This option also allows the viewer to jump to specific points where each person appears. From this section, you can also enable or disable the social interaction in the video by enabling or disabling the comments. Finally, you can upload your own subtitles, if necessary, to provide a transcript of the video in several languages.

Microsoft Stream also provides an editing feature that is handy for trimming Microsoft Teams recordings. To edit the final videos of your meetings, do the following:

1. Open Microsoft Stream in the browser by going to `https://web.microsoftstream.com/`.

2. On the menu, click on **My content** and then **Meetings**.

3. Under the actions, click on ....

4. In the submenu, click on **Trim Video**:

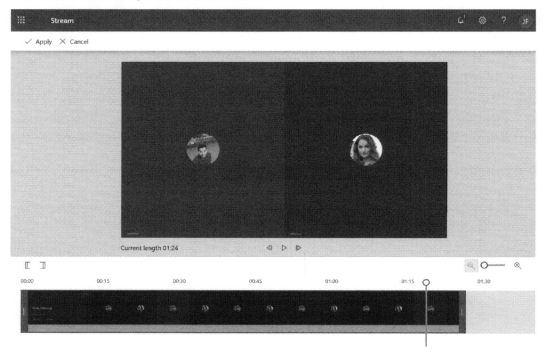

Figure 4.30: Trim video

5. Drag and drop the left and right selectors to define the beginning and the end of the video.

6. Once you are happy with the result, click **Apply**. The original video will be replaced by the new shortest version.

> **Note**
> Microsoft Stream does not allow you to split a video and create a final video using multiple subsections of the original video. To do something like that, you will need to download the video, edit it using a third-party tool, and replace the original video with the new one.

The meeting recordings always start with a screen displaying information related to the meetings and the video itself. On the first frames of the video, you will see the title of the meeting, the date, including the time zone, the name of the organizer, and the name of the presenter who clicked on the record button, as shown in the following screenshot:

Figure 4.31: Meeting recording start screen

How to take meeting notes

Meeting notes are always available during a meeting. However, they are not immediately visible when the meeting starts. To take notes, do the following:

1. During the meeting, click on the three dots (**...**) in the Personal meeting control bar.

2. In the submenu, click on **Show meeting notes**.

3. By default, the notes are displayed in the right pane, as shown in the following screenshot, but you can make them fullscreen if you click on the **View notes tab** link:

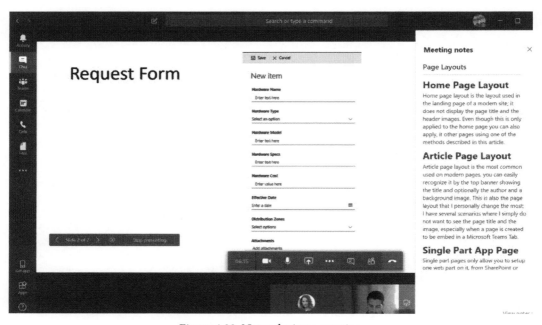

Figure 4.32: Notes during a meeting

Managing meeting notes, files, and whiteboards

During a meeting, you can share or produce different types of content, namely notes, files, or whiteboards. Each add value to the meeting, not just when it is occurring, but also once it finishes as all this material continues to be available so that it can be consulted in the context of the meeting where it was produced or shared.

To open a meeting and access the content produced during a Teams meeting, you can use the recent section in the chat app, as we saw previously, or you can use the search feature. Once you've found the desired meeting and clicked on it, you will get access to all its contents, including the chat.

The following screenshot shows all the meeting tabs that give you access to the assets highlighted. Each of the tabs will display the corresponding content on the stage area and you will be able to modify or share it with someone else:

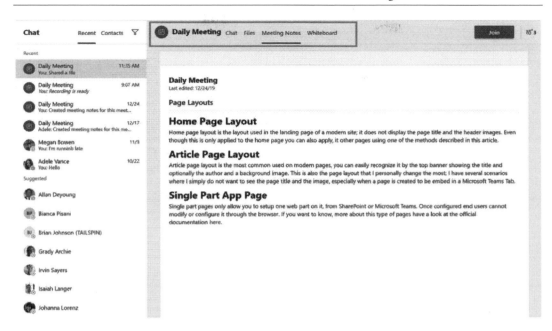

Figure 4.33: Notes after a meeting

Meetings on the mobile app

If you are on the go and need to attend a Microsoft Teams meeting, you can do so using the mobile app on your phone. The meeting options are not the same ones you have when joining using the computer, but you will still be able to interact with the other participants and see all the content being shared.

To join a meeting using the mobile version of Teams, you need to do the following:

1. Open Teams and tap **Calendar**.

2. From the agenda, choose the meeting you want to attend and tap **Join**.

3. Once connected, to get access to the meeting controls, you can tap anywhere on the screen.

Even though the screen is smaller, most of the options that you can find in the desktop version are just one tap away. The following screenshots highlight the features available when using a mobile phone to attend a meeting:

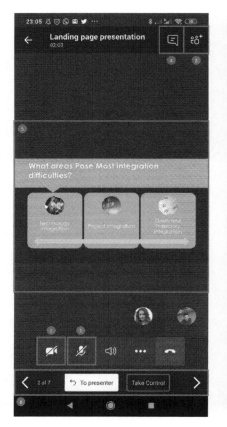

Figure 4.34: Microsoft Teams meeting mobile view

These features are as follows:

1. Turn on/off the video using your cellphone cameras.

2. Mute/Unmute yourself.

3. Add people to the meeting.

4. Access the chat and share files.

5. To view the content being shared, you can pinch to zoom in/out.

6. Take control of a PowerPoint presentation.

7. Share your mobile phone screen.

When sharing your screen from a mobile device, a red rectangle will be added to identify the area being shared. At any given time, you can open other apps without disconnecting the call. The Microsoft Teams mobile app will continue to record everything on the screen. The following screenshot illustrates what mobile sharing looks like to other participants in the call using the desktop version of Teams:

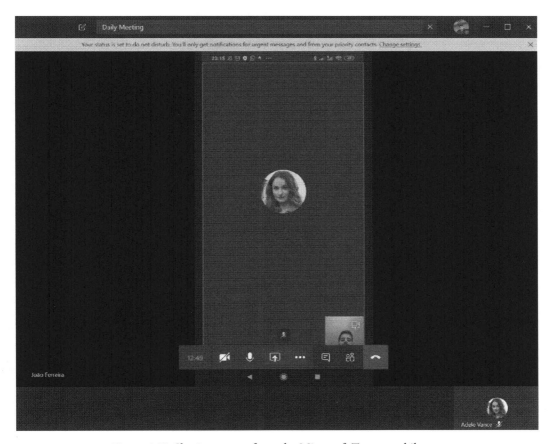

Figure 4.35: Sharing screen from the Microsoft Teams mobile app

Occasionally, meetings go over the scheduled time or you simply have a schedule conflict and cannot be on the computer for the entire meeting. Microsoft Teams has a built-in feature to help you with scenarios like this, which allows you to switch from the desktop to your mobile device so that you can continue the meeting with no downtime and work on the go.

To transfer meetings between devices, do the following:

1. While connected to the meeting on your computer, open Microsoft Teams on your phone and tap the **Calendar**.

2. At the top of the app, you will see a message with a **Join** button and a message stating **Join to share content from this device**, as shown in the following screenshot. Tap the **Join** button:

Figure 4.36: Joining a meeting from the Microsoft Teams mobile app

3. Disconnect from the meeting on your computer and you are good to go!

Managing meetings as an admin

Some of the meeting options described in this chapter can be controlled by the admin and might not be available for everyone in the organization. This section covers what you need to know about meetings from the administrator's perspective.

Meeting features are managed through policies and can be applied to users individually. This means that you can enable different features for different users.

To manage existent meeting policies or create new ones, do the following:

1. Open **Microsoft Teams admin center.** You can do this by opening the Microsoft 365 Admin Center and then choosing Teams or by simply going to the following URL: `https://admin.teams.microsoft.com`

2. On the left menu, click on **Meetings** and then **Meeting policies**:

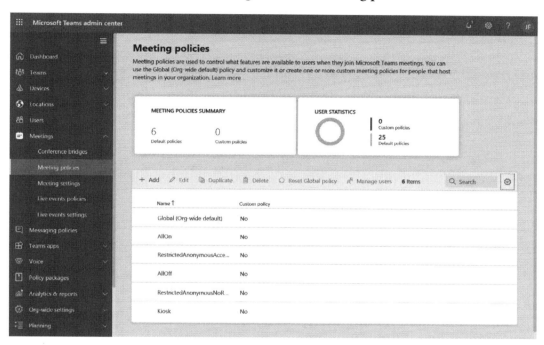

Figure 4.37: Meeting policies

3. To create a new policy, click on **Add**. To manage an existing one, click on one of the policy's names.

4. Each policy is defined by a name, a description, and a bunch of settings that are divided into four different groups that allow you to turn on/off meeting features. The following screenshots illustrate each of the groups and their respective features. Let's take a look:

- **General**: In this group, you will find the general settings for the meeting related to scheduling:

Figure 4.38: General meeting options

- **Audio and video**: In this group, you will find settings related to the audio and video that are used during a Teams meeting:

Figure 4.39: Audio and video options

- **Content sharing**: In this group, you will find settings for the different types of content that can be used during a Teams meeting that are held in your organization:

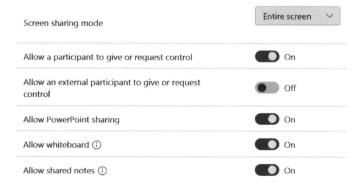

Figure 4.40: Content sharing options

- **Participants and guests**: In this group, you will find participant and guest settings that allow you to control access to Teams meetings:

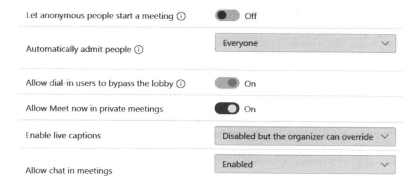

Figure 4.41: Participant's options

Each newly created policy needs to be applied to users to take effect. To apply a new policy to an existing user, do the following:

1. Once in the **Microsoft Teams admin center**, click on **Users**, located in the left menu.

2. Select the users you want to apply the new policy to.

3. Click on **Edit settings**.

4. Change the desired policy, as shown in the following screenshot:

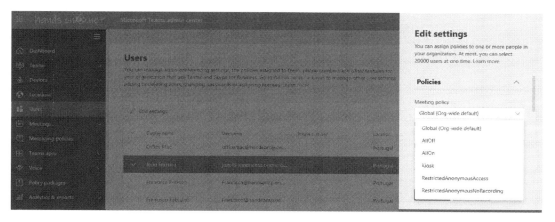

Figure 4.42: Appling a meeting policy to users

5. Click on **Save**.

We have now understood how to create, schedule, and customize meetings. In the next section, we will see how to set up an audio conference in Microsoft Teams meetings.

Audio Conferencing

Audio Conferencing is an add-on to Microsoft Teams that allow users to join meetings by dialing a number from their phones. This feature is included with the Office 365 E5 plan, but on Office 365 E1 and E3, it is sold separately.

Audio Conferencing comes in handy in a variety of scenarios, such as the following:

- When the meeting is audio only.
- The user doesn't have access to a computer or a mobile phone with the Microsoft Teams app installed.
- The network bandwidth is not good enough for audio to be used.

The custom license for Audio Conferencing is only necessary for those users who will schedule meetings. Users attending meetings are not required to have the same license.

> **Note**
> Audio Conferencing is not available in all countries. To check if it is available in your region, go to `https://docs.microsoft.com/en-us/ microsoftteams/country-and-region-availability- for-audio-conferencing-and-calling-plans/country- and-region-availability-for-audio-conferencing- and-calling-plans.`

When a user has an Audio Conferencing license assigned to them, the meeting request that's sent for any meeting will include the dial-in details, as shown in the following screenshot:

Join Microsoft Teams Meeting

+1 437-703-4268   Canada, Toronto (Toll)

Conference ID: 607 334 911#

Local numbers | Reset PIN | Learn more about Teams | Meeting options

Figure 4.43: Meeting request with dial-in options

The meeting request will show a default number, but the participant has the ability to use a local number. The list of local numbers is available through the **Local numbers** link in the meeting request. Once a participant dials the phone number, they will be asked to introduce the conference ID so that they can be connected to the correct meeting.

Audio Conferencing for administrators

Audio Conferencing might require configuration from the Microsoft Teams administrator in order to get the call information in the meeting requests. In this section, you will find basic instructions that will help you get started with the Audio Conferencing and conferencing bridge configurations.

To configure Audio Conferencing, do the following:

1. Open the Microsoft 365 Admin Center.

2. In the left navigation bar, go to **Voice** and then **Phone numbers**.

3. Click on **Add**. The options beyond this point might be different, depending on the country you select. The following screenshot includes the fields for Portugal.

4. Provide an order name and a friendly description.

5. Select your country.

6. Select the number type. Microsoft Teams uses different number types, depending on how you plan to use them in your organization:

    (a) **Call queue (Toll)**: These are service numbers that are used when you are creating a call queue and will be used on resource accounts.

    (b) **Call queue (Toll Free)**: These are service numbers that are used when you are creating a call queue and will be used on resource accounts.

    (c) **Auto attendant (Toll)**: These are service numbers that are used when you are creating an auto attendant and will be assigned to a resource account.

    (d) **Auto attendant (Toll Free)**: These are service numbers that are used when you are creating an auto attendant and will be assigned to a resource account.

    (e) **Dedicated conference bridge (Toll)**: These are service numbers that are used on conference bridges so that users can dial in to meetings.

    (f) **Dedicated conference bridge (Toll Free)**: These are service numbers that are used on conference bridges so that users can dial in to meetings.

7. Fill in all the other options in the form, as shown in the following screenshot:

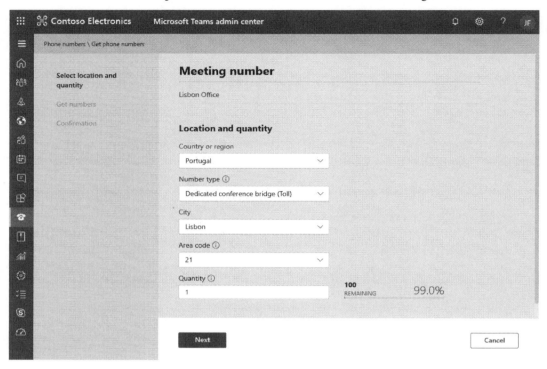

Figure 4.44: New meeting number

8. Click on **Next** and wait for a number to be assigned to you.

9. If everything looks OK with your number, click on **Place order**. You have 10 minutes to do this, after which the number will return to the pool of available numbers:

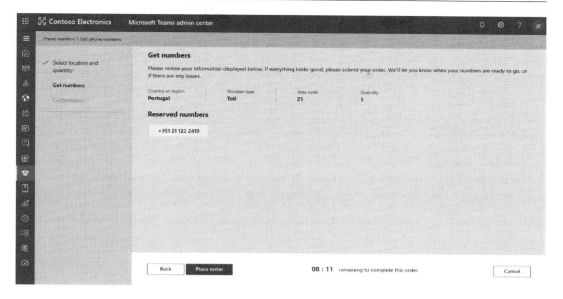

Figure 4.45: Placing a number order

10. Click on **Finish**.

Now that you have your new number to use, it is time to configure the Audio Conferencing bridge. A conferencing bridge is the hub for your phone numbers and can contain one or multiple numbers for multiple countries.

The numbers included in the Conferencing Bridge are the ones that will be included in the meeting request. Bridges can have two types of numbers:

- **Dedicated**: Numbers available for users inside the organization
- **Shared**: Numbers that can be shared with another organization

> **Note**
>
> Once the organization has been enabled for Audio Conferencing, numbers for different countries are automatically assigned, but you can modify the Conferencing Bridge and add more numbers.

1. Open the Microsoft 365 Admin Center.
2. In the left navigation bar, go to **Meetings** and then **Conference bridges**.

3.   Click on **Add** and select the type of number you wish to use:

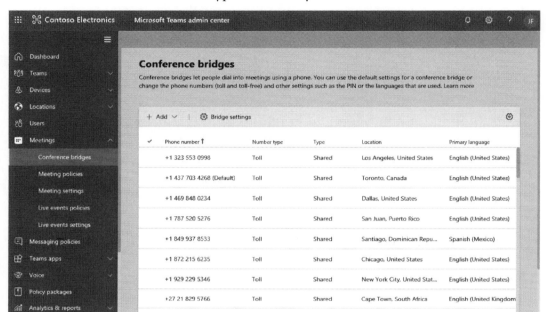

Figure 4.46: Adding a new conference bridge

4.   Select the number from the list and click **Apply**.

Now that Audio Conferencing has been configured, your users can include the call information in the meeting. We will now move on to configuring live events in Microsoft Teams.

Live events on Microsoft Teams

Live events on Microsoft Teams are an extension of meetings and should be used every time you have the need to broadcast for a large audience. Meetings on Microsoft Teams only supports 250 attendees. If you are planning a meeting that exceeds this number, you must use live events instead, which supports up to 10,000 attendees.

Live events are, by definition, a one-to-many communication since the presenters have the rights to speak and share content and all the other attendees can only listen and interact with the presenters through the moderated Q&A.

Live event profiles

By reading the live events introduction, you can probably tell that it might be too complicated for a single person to manage everything that happens during the event. If you have had this thought, then you are right: when looking at live events, you will find four different profiles:

- **Organizer**: This is the person who is responsible for scheduling and inviting presenters and producers to the event and is also responsible for defining the live event permissions. Once the event is over, the organizer will get access to the final reports showing the attendees and the questions that were asked during the event.

- **Presenter**: As the name suggests, the presenter will have the rights to present video, audio, or a desktop window. A live event can have one or more presenters.

- **Producer**: A producer is responsible for starting and stopping the live event, as well as managing everything related to the media presentation, including selecting what video is going live at any moment.

- **Attendee**: An attendee can watch the event and participate through the moderated Q&A. Live events allow attendees to join using authenticated means or anonymously, depending on the event's permissions.

The full experience of live events is only accessible to all profiles through the desktop version of Microsoft Teams. If you are a producer or a presenter, it is mandatory to use the desktop client. If you are an attendee, you can join using the desktop, web, or mobile clients of Teams.

How to create a live event

Live events must be created on Microsoft Teams, and the process is similar to scheduling a meeting. To create a live event, do the following:

1. On the desktop Teams client, open the **Calendar**.
2. Click on the arrow next to the **New meeting** button.

3.   On the popup, select **New live event**. By default, **New meeting** is selected:

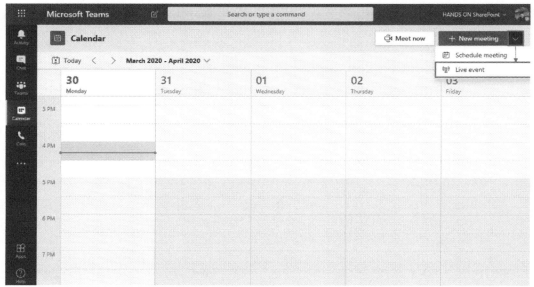

Figure 4.47: New live event

4.   Fill in the form with the event's details.

5.   Define your role for the event.

6.   Invite other producers and presenters. The organizer can assume one of these two roles:

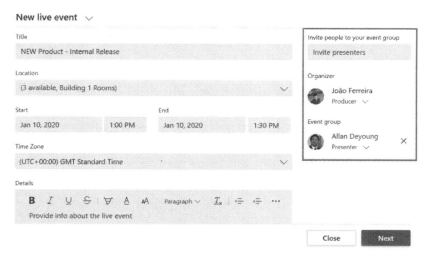

Figure 4.48: Presenters and producers

7. Click **Next**.

8. Select the event permissions. Here, you will find three different options, as follows:

    (a) **People and Groups**: As the event organizer, you need to invite the people and groups that will have permission to watch the event.

    (b) **Org-wide**: Everyone in the organization will have access to the event, and the attendees will be identified by the corporate account. Org-wide events require the user to sign in.

    (c) **Public**: Everyone with the link will be able to join without authentication:

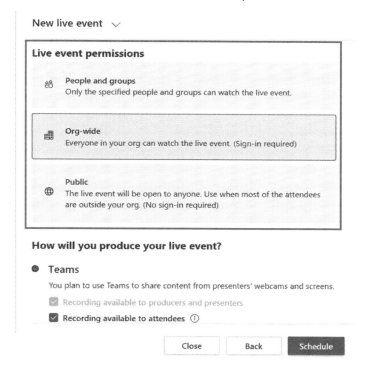

Figure 4.49: Live event permissions

9. Select the production options for the event. Here, you can choose Teams or a third-party app or device. If you select Teams, there are a few settings you can configure for the live event and for the content generated after it, as follows:

    (a) **Record availability**: You can select the profiles that the recording will be available to after the meeting. Depending on the configurations made by the administrator, one or more options can be locked or not even exist. To find out more, please read the *Managing live events as an admin* section.

(b) **Captions**: During the event, you can enable captions for the attendees to follow. To use this option, you will have to define the spoken language. From here, you will be able to select up to six different languages for the captions.

(c) **Attendee engagement report**: This option generates a report of the behavior of the attendees during the live event.

(d) **Q&A**: This option enables a Q&A session during the live event. Attendees will be able to ask a question and the presenter or the producer will be able to reply to it privately or publicly:

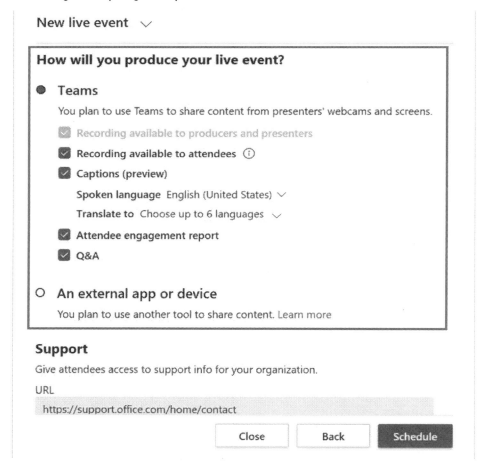

Figure 4.50: Production options

10. Define the URL for the support. The default value can be modified by the administrator.

11. Click on **Schedule**.

12. Once scheduled, you will see the details of the event with the option to get an attendee link that you can use to invite people to the event, for example, through a newsletter or a blog post:

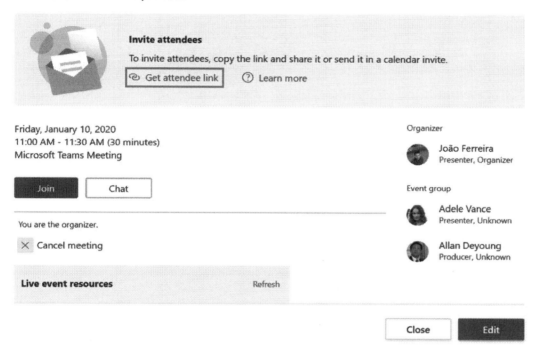

Figure 4.51: Get attendee link

What are the available options during a live event?

Live events will be displayed differently, depending of the participant role, and show different screens with different options for each of them.

Unlike meetings, live events have the possibility for dry runs to be performed so as to make sure that everything works as expected once the event goes live. Only producers and presenters have access to this pre-live stage of the event. If an attendee joins the event during the pre-live, they will wait in a virtual lobby until the event starts.

Producer

The following screenshot represents the screen of a producer during the pre-live stage, with the main options highlighted:

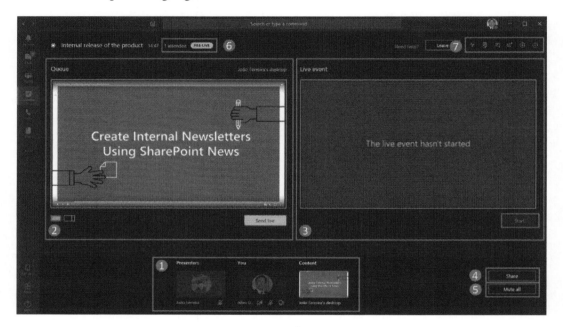

Figure 4.52: Producer view

Let's explain each of these options:

1. **Content selector**: In this section, you will see all the presenters and the content being shared. Once you click on the content, it is sent to the queue. In this section, you will also see yourself and your controls for the camera and microphone.

2. **Queue**: This is the preview of the content waiting to be sent live. Here, you can see how things will look before sending them to the event.

3. **Live event**: An image of what is being shared in the event at the moment. This section only displays content once you've sent something from the queue to the live event. To start a live event, it is mandatory to have something already being shared, otherwise the **Start** button will remain disabled, as shown in the preceding screenshot.

4. **Share**: The producer also has the option to share content from your computer. If you want to do so, click on the **Share** button.

5. **Mute all**: The producer has the option to mute all the participants in the live event. If you have the need to do this, press the **Mute all** button.

6. **Live event information**: In this section, you will get information about the status of the event and the number of attendees. The attendees counter will work even if you are not live yet. This will let you know how many attendees are waiting for it to start.

7. **Personal and event options**: In this section, you will find your personal settings for the event, such as the option to configure the microphone and webcams. These options are available when you press the cog well. In this bar, you will also find options for the event, such as Q&A, notes, and chat, among others. The first icon in this group is a tool that you can use to monitor the status of your internet connection before going live to make sure you have sufficient bandwidth to stream and manage the content:

Bonus tip

Microsoft Teams marks the event with a yellow label when it is not live and wraps the content that is not live with a yellow border. Once the event is live, a red label is added to the event and the content being shared is marked with a red border. If you are a visual person, this will definitely help you understand what is live and what is not.

Figure 4.53: Producer Q&A

8. **Q&A**: The Q&A is displayed in the right pane on Microsoft Teams and will indicate whether it's enabled for the event. You can get access to it by clicking the second button shown for the event options.

9. **Question groups**: The questions you receive during a live event are private and are organized into three different groups, as shown in the preceding screenshot. They are moved to the groups when you publish or dismiss them.

10. **Q&A status**: The producer has the option to decide when to open the Q&A. If you do not want to have it open during the entire event, you can use this toggle to close it.

11. **Questions queue**: In this section, you will be able to see all the questions sent during the event, reply to them, publish them to everyone, and see or dismiss them. You also have the option to reply to a question without publishing it. Private replies are labeled private with a locker icon and will only be shared with the attendee who made it.

12. **Make an announcement**: The announcement option allows you to write on the Q&A panel for the attendees.

When you click on the start button, Microsoft Teams will show a warning message to inform users that a live event cannot exceed 4 hours. Attendees will see it with a 10-20 second delay:

Are you sure you want to start the live event now?

Once you start, you can't stop and restart. The event can last up to 4 hours from start time and attendees will watch at a 10-20 second delay. Learn more

Figure 4.54: Starting a live event

Presenter

The presenter options during a live event are the same as the ones explained previously in the *What are the available options during a meeting?* section.

Compared to the options available during a meeting, the presenter loses the ability to share a PowerPoint presentation directly and share whiteboards. The UI also gets two new options, which are highlighted in the following screenshot:

Figure 4.55: Presenter controls

These options are as follows:

1. **Status**: This label allows you to understand what the status of the event is using three different words mapped with colors:

    Pre-Live: Yellow

    Live: Red

    Ended: Gray

2. **Q&A**: Opens the Q&A panel in the right pane. The presenter has the same controls as the producer when it comes to managing the questions that are sent by the attendees.

Attendee

Attendees only have the option to view the content being shared and, if enabled, interact with the presenters and producers through the Q&A. The following screenshot demonstrates what the window looks like to an attendee during the live event:

Figure 4.56: Attendee view

There are two areas here, as follows:

1. **Stage**: In this area, the attendee will see the content being shared and have the option to leave the event if they want to.

2. **Q&A**: The Q&A panel is also displayed in the right panel but with limited options. An attendee will be able to see their own questions and the replies to them and the ones that the producer or the presenter have made public by publishing them. An attendee has the option to make anonymous questions. To do this, they just need to check the box under the text area.

Getting live event reports and the recording

A live event produces a video of the recording and a series of reports that you can use to analyze the behavior of the attendees and measure the success of the event.

The organizer and the presenters will have access to this data through Microsoft Teams once the event is over.

To download them, do the following:

1. Open Microsoft Teams and click on the Calendar.

2. Click on the live event on the Calendar.

3. On the event popup, scroll to the **Live event resources** section:

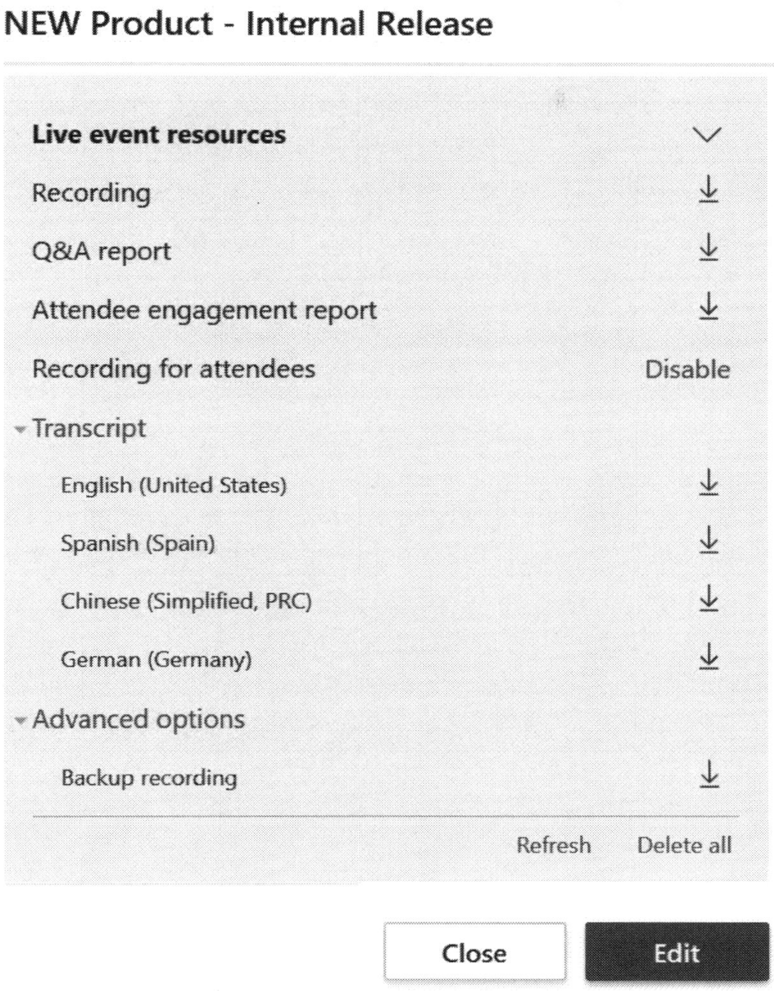

NEW Product - Internal Release

Figure 4.57: Live event resources

For each live event, Microsoft Teams can produce several types of resources, and all of them must be downloaded to be viewed:

- **Videos**: Each live event produces two recordings so that in case something goes wrong, there is always a backup available. Videos are produced using the mp4 video format.

- **Reports**: After the event, Microsoft Teams generates two reports, one with all the questions that were asked during the event, and another with the behavior of the attendees during the event. Both reports are produced using the CSV file format and can be viewed using Excel, as shown in the following screenshot:

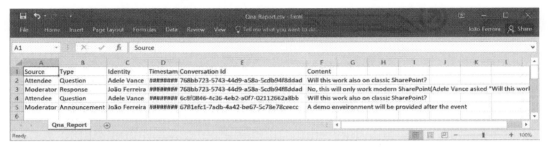

Figure 4.58: Live event report

- **Transcripts**: Transcripts are the subtitles you can add to your videos. Microsoft Teams produces transcripts for all the languages selected when the event is first created (up to six). The transcripts are produced using the VTT file format.

The recordings from a live event are not stored in Microsoft Stream, but you can use the generated video file and transcripts to upload them and make them available on the media platform.

You can distinguish between a live event on a Microsoft Teams Calendar from a meeting by looking at the antenna icon that the live event displays:

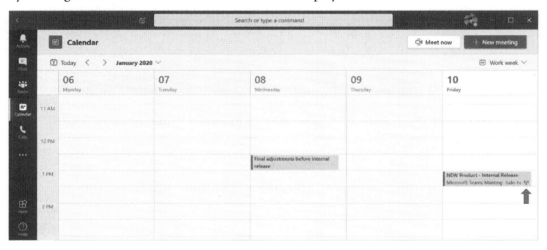

Figure 4.59: Live event icon

Managing live events as an admin

You may not see all the options described in this chapter for live events; some of them can be controlled by the administrator using policies.

If you are an administrator and want to enable or disable live event features, do the following:

1. Open **Microsoft Teams admin center**. You can do this by opening the Microsoft 365 Admin Center and then choosing **Teams** or by simply opening the following URL: `https://admin.teams.microsoft.com`

2. On the left menu, click on **Meetings** and then **Live events policies**:

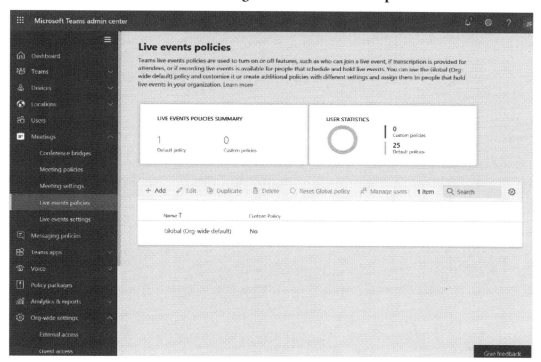

Figure 4.60: Live event policies

3. To create a new policy, click on **Add**. To manage an existing one, click one of the policy's names.

Each policy is defined by a name, a description, and four settings that allow you to turn on/off features and define who has access to live events, as illustrated in the following screenshot:

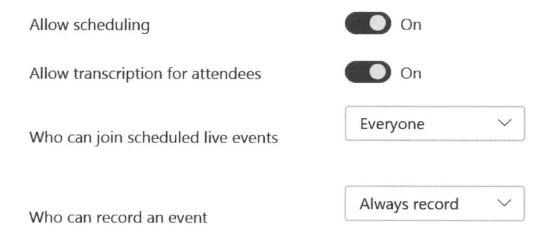

Figure 4.61: Live event policy options

By clicking the **Who can join scheduled live events** setting, you will see three different options that will restrict the options available when scheduling the event:

- **Everyone**: All users, including external and anonymous users, will have permission to join the live event. To create public live events, this option must be selected.

- **Everyone in the organization**: All users from your organization will be able to join the live event.

- **Specific users or groups**: You will have to define the users or groups who will have access to the live event when scheduling.

By clicking the **Who can record an event** option, you will see that three options are available:

- **Always record**: The video will always be recorded, and the organizer and the presenters will have access to it once the meeting is finished.

- **Never record**: The live event will not be recorded.

- **Organizer can record**: The organizer has the option to decide whether the live event is recorded.

Meetings and live events limitations

Live events and meetings features have a few limitations that you should be aware of before using them. In the following table, you will find the important limit numbers that you should take into consideration when choosing between meetings and live events.

Please note that as Microsoft Teams evolves, these numbers may increase:

	Meetings	Live Events
Max number of people	250	10,000
Max length	NA	4h
Max number of concurrent events	NA	15
Max PowerPoint file size	2 GB	NA
Max streaming resolution	NA	720p
Max number of presenters	NA	10
Max number of people using Audio Conferencing	250	NA

Summary

In this chapter, you have learned how to use Microsoft Teams to schedule meetings and organize live events using all the features included in the product. You were provided with a full description of all the features included in both functionalities and are now ready to decide when to use each of them.

In the next chapter, you will learn how to protect information inside Microsoft Teams using private channels and what they mean in Teams.

5
Public versus Private – Teams and Channels

In the first chapter of this book, we covered the basics of all the Microsoft Teams components and the general usage scenarios for teams, channels, and tabs.

In this chapter, we will dive into the teams and channels features included on Microsoft Teams. We will look at the differences between the several types of teams and channels that are available, with scenarios that will help you understand what the best approach to follow is, based on your requirements.

In the following pages, you will find information about these main topics:

- Understanding public and private teams
- Understanding standard channels
- Understanding private channels
- Understanding team creation governance
- Organizing your teams and channels
- Understanding team and channel limits

Understanding public and private teams

When creating a new team, you have the option to make it public or private, but before making that decision you need to be aware of the differences between both types.

A public team is discoverable to all members of an organization and is listed in the Teams gallery.

> **A public team scenario—Peter the office manager**
>
> Peter is responsible for managing the company office in Portugal. To do it better and to communicate with others, Peter has created a new team for the office where he posts everything related to it. Anyone working in Portugal or visiting the office can join the team to access things such as the location and working hours, or simply to ask Peter or any of the other office members something.

A private team can be discoverable or non-discoverable. Also, to be a member of a team, you need to either be approved or added to the team. If the team is discoverable, you can request to join it; if it's non-discoverable, a team owner needs to add you.

> **A private team scenario—company managers**
>
> The HANDS ON tek company has a private team for all company managers where new acquisitions are discussed. The information in this team is private and must not be discovered by any user. Every time a new manager is hired or promoted, they are added to the team by one of the owners.

Keep in mind the two scenarios described in this section every time you have doubts about what type of team you should create.

In the next section, we will learn what guest users on Microsoft Teams are and how they are related to the public and private concepts.

Guest users on Microsoft Teams

Don't get misled by the type of a team; public teams don't mean that you will be able to add guest users to them by default. In fact, you are able to add users from other organizations to your teams when using public and private teams. All you have to do is enable the guest access on your tenant. Guest access can be only enabled by the Microsoft Teams global administrator and once enabled, everyone can use it.

If you have the right permissions and want to enable guest access to your organization, do the following:

1. Open the Microsoft Teams admin center (`https://admin.teams.microsoft.com`).

2. In the left-hand side menu, click on **Org-wide settings** and then on **Guest access**.

3. Switch the **Allow guest access in Teams** toggle to **On**.

4. Configure the available features for **Calling**, **Meeting**, and **Messaging** that guest users will be able to use on your tenant, as in the following screenshot:

Figure 5.1: Enabling guest access on Microsoft Teams

5. Click **Save**.

Once this feature is enabled, you can add users from other organizations to your teams. When doing so, you will notice that Microsoft Teams displays a message showing that the user is a guest, as in the following screenshot:

Figure 5.2: Adding a guest member to a team

All teams with guest users will also display a label at the top of the screen showing the number of guest members that exist in the team, as in the following screenshot:

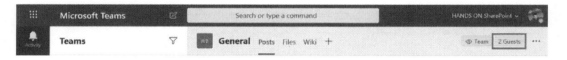

Figure 5.3: Guest information

Guest access allows the creation of real multi-organizational environments on Microsoft Teams. Any user with an email account can be added to the team to collaborate and be able to access files, meetings, and chats.

> **Important note: Guest access checklist**
>
> In order to enable guest access in Microsoft Teams, it must also be enabled in Azure Active Directory, Office 365 groups, and SharePoint. To make sure your tenant is prepared to be accessed by guest users, validate the checklist at the following site:
>
> `https://docs.microsoft.com/en-us/microsoftteams/`
> `guest-access-checklist`

Understanding standard channels

Standard channels were, until recently, the only available way of creating a channel inside a team. Standard channels, as seen in *Chapter 1, Microsoft Teams Basics*, are subsets of a team and are used to have conversations and share documents on the same topic.

Everything shared in a standard channel becomes available to all the team members. However, this was, for a long time, a major limitation to Microsoft Teams, forcing channel owners to duplicate their teams in order to share private and sensitive information.

> **A standard channel scenario—John the teacher**
>
> John is a teacher responsible for an eighth-grade class and a strong advocate of Microsoft Teams. He wants to build an e-learning platform for his class using Teams. This platform will be publicly available to all the class students and teachers.
>
> John has created a standard channel for each school subject and added all the teachers and the students to the team using their school accounts. John has structured the team but is now facing an issue with the **Teachers** standard channel, which may contain information that should not be available to students.

The following screenshot shows how this scenario will look when implemented:

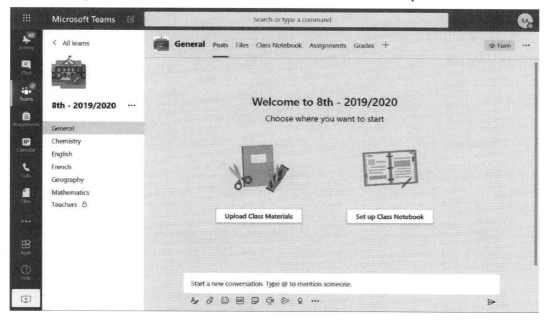

Figure 5.4: John's team structure

This is the typical channel scenario you will find in Microsoft Teams and is also a perfect example of how private channels are handy when you need to target information within the same team. The **Teachers** channel should be a private place where all the teachers can share private information about the students. Let's see how this works in the next section.

> **Note**
>
> The scenario represented in this section of the book uses an education tenant. Education tenants include all the main features and components that are included in the standard version of Microsoft Teams; however, they have different layouts to manage teams and include specific user profiles for users, such as teacher and student. I have not covered this tenant in this book as it has special features that are only available for education. However, more information about Microsoft Teams education tenants can be found at `https://support.microsoft.com/en-us/office/microsoft-teams-5aa4431a-8a3c-4aa5-87a6-b6401abea114?ui=en-US&rs=en-US&ad=US#ID0EAABAAA=About`.

Understanding private channels

Private channels were the most requested feature ever since Microsoft Teams was released, with more than 25,000 requests for it to be implemented. It took almost 3 years for them to be publicly available:

Welcome to the Microsoft Teams UserVoice!

← Public

25,140 votes

Vote

Support for Private Channels

Private channels enable focused private collaboration among a subset of your team...

Angela Sze shared this idea · November 01, 2016 · Flag idea as inappropriate.

COMPLETED · **Alex** (Teams Engineering, Microsoft Teams) responded · November 07, 2019

Private channels enable focused private collaboration among a subset of your team. We are super excited to share that this feature is fully rolled out to the public ring. You can find detailed information on the capabilities and management of the private channels feature here – https://docs.microsoft.com/MicrosoftTeams/private-channels.

Figure 5.5: A user voice request

A private channel has pretty much the same functionalities as a standard channel. The main differences between the two are individual site collections and special permissions are not inherited from the team.

What is a site collection?

A site collection on SharePoint is a container for a group of sites, files, or pages that has its own permissions. A site collection starts with a top-level site and can contain other subsites underneath.

A private channel scenario—Geno the basketball coach

Geno is a college basketball coach who uses Microsoft Teams to manage everything related to his team. He has created several channels inside his team that are publicly available to athletes, coaches, and staff members.

Geno likes to keep information centralized for better management and faster access, so he is looking for a solution that allows him to discuss and share private information with his assistant coaches.

Private channels are the correct solution for this scenario and Geno has created two private channels inside the team to discuss the following:
• Athletes' scouting
• Athletes' calls for upcoming games

By following this approach, Geno was able to keep the information centralized and at the same time, keep sensitive data private and hidden from the rest of the team.

How to create a private channel

The creation of private channels is only available to members of the organization. As a user, when you create a new private channel, you will be made the owner of the channel automatically.

To create a new private channel in your teams, do the following:

1. Hover over the name of the team where you want to create the private channel and click on **...** next to the name.

2. From the options menu, click on **Add channel**:

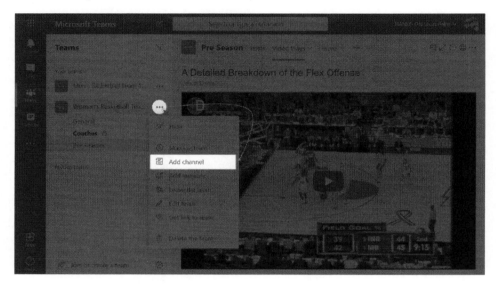

Figure 5.6: Adding a channel

3. In the creation form, provide a name and a description to help identify the channel and select **Private** in the **Privacy** dropdown:

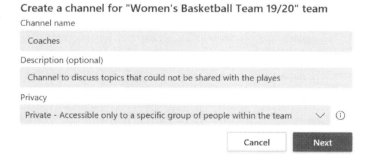

Figure 5.7: Creating a private channel

4. Click **Next.**

5. Add members to the channel and select their roles (either members or owners). Optionally, you can skip this step and add them later.

6. Even though a site collection is created with the new private channel, it will be available for use in just a few seconds.

7. The URL for the private channel site collection is a combination of the name of the team and the name of the channel; for example, `https://handsontek.sharepoint.com/sites/hr-vacations`. Looking at the URL of this site collection, we can tell that it belongs to the *Vacations* private channel in the *HR* team.

Private channels can only be created. Due to their special structure, it is not possible to transform an existent standard channel into a private channel.

The structure and features of private channels

Private channels have a different physical structure to standard channels. If you create a private channel, keep in mind that each new channel generates a new site collection with different permissions for the team.

Each team on Microsoft Teams creates a new site collection and each standard channel creates a folder inside a document library. When a new private channel is created, instead of getting a new folder in the document library, you will get a new site collection, where all your files and conversations will be stored.

The following diagram shows the physical structure of a team with standard channels versus a team with private channels:

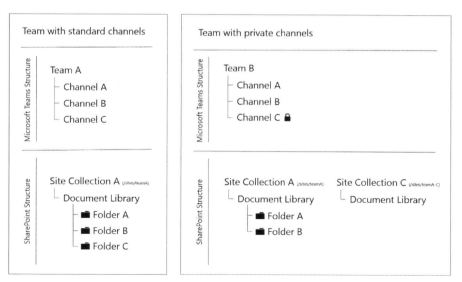

Figure 5.8: Microsoft Teams versus SharePoint physical structure

Even though a private channel creates a new SharePoint site collection, you should not plan to use it as a regular site. Site collections associated with private channels do not allow the creation of pages; you will be only able to create libraries and lists.

To support private channels, SharePoint increased the limit of site collections from 500,000 to 2,000,000.

Private channels, when compared to standard channels, are also limited in features. You will be able to access the chat and wiki, but bots and meetings are not available. The following table shows a comparison between standard channels and private channels that will help you to decide which one to use based on the available features:

	Standard channel	Private channel
Channel email	✓	✓
Apps	✓	✓
Bots	✓	✗
External users	✓	✓
Channel meetings	✓	✓
Scheduled channel meetings	✓	✗

Private channels have their own settings and override some of the settings defined by the team. The following table shows a comparison between standard and private channel settings and allows you to understand how each of these settings are overwritten by the private channel:

	Standard channel	Private channel
Member permissions	Team	Channel
Guest permissions	Team	Team
@mentions	Team	Channel
Fun stuff	Team	Channel
Moderation permissions	Channel	N/A

Channel settings are available to the team owners on the standard channels and to the channel owners on the private channels. To access these settings, do the following:

1. Hover over the channel name and then click on **...** to open the options menu.

2. From the options menu, click on **Manage channel**. Depending on the type of the channel, a popup will open with different options:

(a) For standard channels, you will have access to the channel moderation permissions, as in the following screenshot:

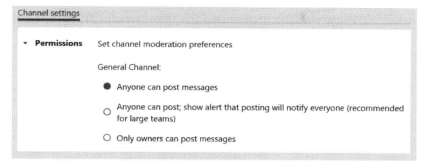

Figure 5.9: Standard channel settings

(b) For private channels, you will have access to the **Member permissions**, **@mentions**, and **Fun stuff** options, as in the following screenshot:

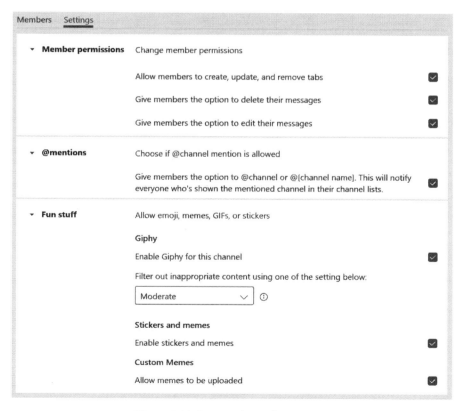

Figure 5.10: Private channel settings

Understanding private channel security

Private channels have their own owners—this means a team owner in the private channel is not necessarily the private channel owner and it is also possible that they are not even part of the private channel. If a team owner does not belong to a private channel, they will be able to see it exists but will not be able to see any of the content inside it.

To become a member of a private channel, a user *must* be a member of a team first. This means that any member of a private channel will have access to all the information in the team.

Private channels also support external users, if they are members of the team already.

An unsupported private channel scenario—Mary the team manager

Mary manages a team of developers in a consulting company that builds custom software based on the customer's requirements. She has a consulting team on Microsoft Teams already and uses it to assign new projects and to share proposals and requirements with the team members.

With the release of private channels, Mary wants to modify the consulting team. She has to do the following:
• Create a private channel for each customer.
• Add the customer as an external member to the private channel.

This scenario is not supported by private channels. To modify the team as Mary wants, she needs to add all her customers to the team where she already has confidential information about all the past projects. By doing this, the customer will be able to see not just the information in the private channel but also the conversations and the files in the standard channels. They will also be able to see who all of Mary's customers are and they will be able to chat with each other.

Pro tip

When working with private channels, do not modify the security settings on the SharePoint site collection. The permissions are managed by Microsoft Teams and they are tightly connected. If you modify the permissions on SharePoint, they will be reverted to the original values automatically to avoid disruption in the private channel functionality.

The following questions will help you understand the privacy policies in private channels with real scenarios that you will face when using Microsoft Teams:

- **What happens when a private channel owner leaves the private channel?**
  When the owner of a private channel leaves the channel, the team, or the company, Microsoft Teams will automatically promote a new team member as the owner of the private channel.

- **Can an external user be a private channel owner?**
  No, an external user will always be a guest in the team and the private channels and cannot be promoted to the channel owner.

- **If a user is removed from a team, will they also be removed from the private channels?**
  If a user is removed from a team, they are removed from all the private channels in the team.

- **Can a team owner view a private channel?**
  Yes, team owners are able to see private channels. As a team owner, if you would like to see all the channels in your team, including the private ones, you should click on the ... option that appears when you hover over the name of a team and then click on **Manage team**. In the stage area, click on the **Channels** tab and you will see all the team channels, as in the following screenshot. Private channels can be identified by the lock icon in the **Type** column:

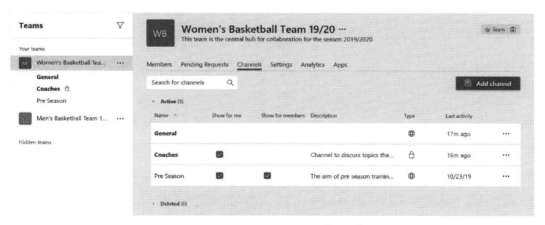

Figure 5.11: Managing team channels

- **Can a team owner access a private channel?**
  No, a team owner will not be able to access a private channel if they are not a member of the channel.

- **Can a team owner delete a private channel?**
  Yes, a team owner will be able to delete a private channel, even if they are not a member of it. This will delete the channel and all its assets.

- **Can a private channel owner leave the channel?**
  Yes, if they are not the last member in the channel. If the member leaving is the only owner, a random member will be assigned as the owner of the private channel.

- **Can a team guest create a private channel?**
  No, private channels can only be created by a member of the organization. Team owners and team members can both create private channels.

The following tables summarize the permissions and actions each profile can have in private channels. Note that in private channels we have a second tier of profiles and it's important to be aware of the different permissions. A team owner will not control everything that happens inside a team if private channels exist:

Action	Team owner	Team member	Team guest
Create a private channel	Yes	Yes	No
Delete a private channel	Yes	No	No
Edit a private channel	No	N/A	N/A
Restore a deleted private channel	Yes	No	No
Add members to a private channel	No	N/A	N/A
Edit the settings of a private channel	No	N/A	N/A
Manage tabs and apps in a private channel	No	N/A	N/A

In the following table, you can how the actions each profile can take are different on private channels:

Action	Private channel owner	Private channel member	Private channel guest
Delete a private channel	Yes	No	No
Leave a private channel	Yes	Yes	Yes
Edit a private channel	Yes	No	No
Restore a deleted private channel	Yes	No	No
Add members	Yes	No	No
Edit settings	Yes	No	No
Manage tabs and apps	Yes	Yes	No

Keep this section of the book in mind and come back to it every time you have doubts about private channels and the level of permissions for each profile.

Understanding team creation governance

Governance is one of the things you should plan carefully. If you have an administrator role, make sure you define a set of rules and configure Teams the way you want ahead of time.

This is no easy task and it will always depend on each individual scenario. You should keep in mind that if you leave everything open, Teams can quickly become a wild west with hundreds of teams and channels that don't make sense. On the other hand, if you adopt a restrictive policy, you may lose users and they will eventually look for alternatives to Microsoft Teams (most likely outside of the Microsoft environment).

This section of the book shows where you can find the teams and channels features that you will be able to manipulate to reach a balance on your Microsoft Teams tenant.

On Microsoft Teams, there is no option to disable the creation of new teams. However, it is possible to disable the creation of Office 365 groups—but it is not recommended to do so as this will have a major impact on other applications.

> **Pro tip**
>
> Don't try to restrict the functionalities on Microsoft Teams unless extremely necessary. Removing features from Microsoft Teams will force your users to use other services that are potentially not secure or compliant with the standards of Microsoft Teams.

Instead of disabling the creation of teams, you can adopt a few practices that will help you manage the teams and, if necessary, restrict the creation of private channels.

Governance as a global Microsoft Teams administrator

As a Microsoft Teams global administrator, you have the power to disable the creation of private channels globally or enable it just for particular users. To do so, you will have to work with **Teams policies** in the **Microsoft Teams admin center**.

To manage **Teams policies** and to attribute them to specific users, do the following:

1. Open the **Microsoft Teams admin center**. You can do this by going to `https://admin.teams.microsoft.com/`.

2. In the left-hand side menu, expand the **Teams** option and then select **Teams policies**:

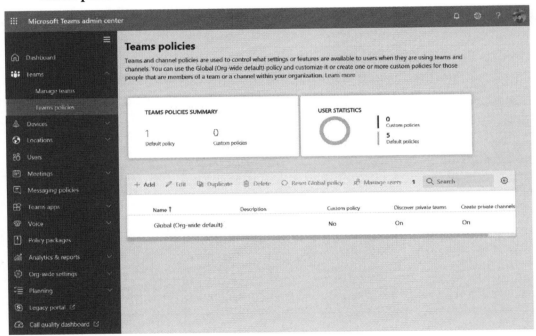

Figure 5.12: Teams policies

3. By default, you will only have the **Global** policy and this is the one that will be applied to all the users in the organization.

4. Select the policy and click on the **Edit** button.

5. The **Global** teams policy has only two settings, which gives you the option to do the following:

    (a) Enable/Disable the discovery of private teams: If the discovery of private teams is enabled, users will be able to find them and request to join.

    (b) Enable/Disable the creation of private channels: This setting allows you to turn off the creation of private channels for the entire organization. When this setting is enabled, a team owner can decide whether members of the team have the right to create private channels.

6. If you want to apply different settings to some of the members of your team to allow them to create private channels, do the following:

    (1) Open the **Microsoft Teams admin center**. You can do so using `https://admin.teams.microsoft.com/`.

    (2) In the left-hand side menu, expand the **Teams** option and then select **Teams policies**.

    (3) Click on **Add**.

    (4) Provide a name and a description that will help you identify your custom policy.

    (5) Define the settings for private team discovery and private channel creation:

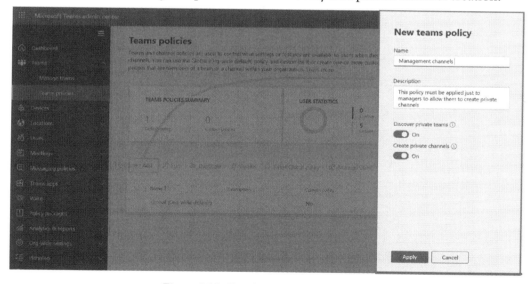

Figure 5.13: Creating a new teams policy

7. Click **Apply**.

8. In the left-hand side menu, click on **Users**.

9. From the list of users, select the ones that you want to apply the new policy to. Selecting more than 20 users at once is not recommended. If your number is greater than 20, you must do it in batches or using PowerShell:

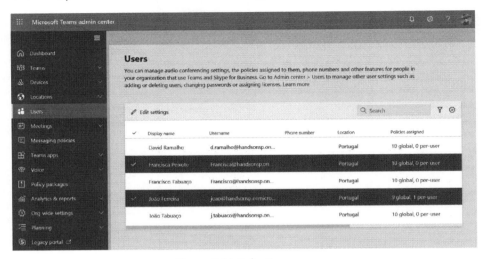

Figure 5.14: Selecting users

10. Click on **Edit settings**.

11. In the right-hand side pane, look for **Teams policy** and select the policy you have just created:

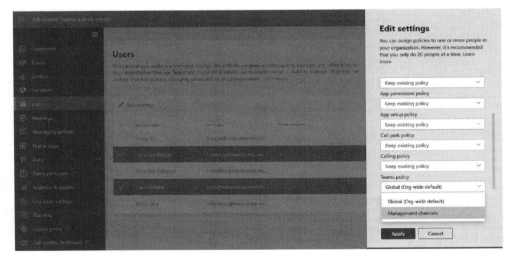

Figure 5.15: Applying a Microsoft Teams policy

12. Click **Apply**. Policies can take up to 24 hours to be applied to users.

Governance as a team owner

If your tenant has the creation of private channels enabled globally for all users, you can fine-tune it for the teams you own. Teams allows you to control who is able to create standard and private channels from the settings of each team.

To disable the creation of standard or private channels by members, do the following:

1. Open the team you want to modify.

2. Click on ... next to the name of the team to expand the options menu.

3. From the menu, click on **Manage team**.

4. Click on the **Settings** tab.

5. Expand **Member permissions**.

6. Uncheck the highlighted settings shown in the following screenshot according to your requirements:

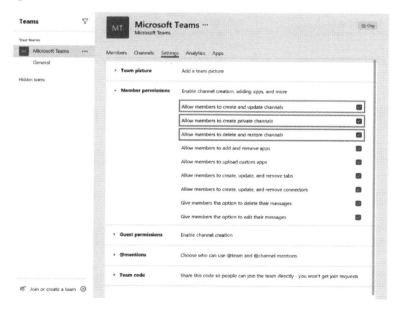

Figure 5.16: Channel settings for team members

> **Note**
>
> If the creation of private channels is disabled by the global admin, you will not be able to enable it as a team owner. If you want to use private channels and for the options under **Member permissions** to look like the following screenshot, you must contact your Microsoft Teams administrator:

Allow members to create private channels

Private channel creation permissions require channel creation to be enabled as well.

Figure 5.17: Private channels disabled by the global administrator

Guest members in your teams can also create or delete channels. However, this feature is not enabled by default, but any team owner can enable it by doing the following:

1. Open the team you want to modify.

2. Click on **...** next to the name of the team to expand the options menu.

3. From the menu, click on **Manage team**.

4. Click on the **Settings** tab.

5. Expand **Guest permissions**.

6. Enable the options highlighted in the following screenshot:

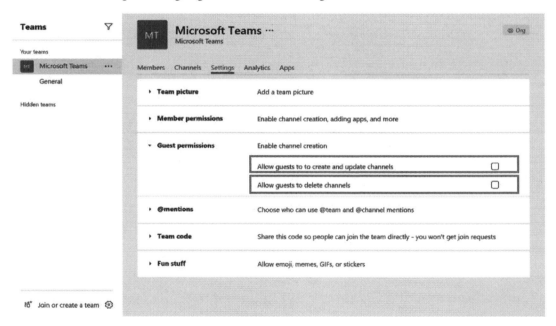

Figure 5.18: Channel settings for guest permissions

Archiving and deleting teams

When using Microsoft Teams, you will end up with a lot of teams and channels that are no longer needed. To better use the platform, you can decide between archiving and deleting them permanently.

> **An archived teams scenario—Geno the basketball coach**
>
> Geno was the main coach of a basketball team during the 2019/2020 season. The season was a success and Geno and his team were the state runners-up. Now that the season is over, Geno no longer needs this team and will archive it. All the content that was shared during the season will remain on the Microsoft servers but the activity will cease.

When a team is archived, all the standard and private channels are archived with it, including the dedicated site collections. To archive one of your teams, you need to open the **Manage teams** panel in Microsoft Teams by doing the following:

1. In the **Manage teams** panel of Microsoft Teams, click on the cog icon at the bottom of the left pane.

2. Expand the **Active** pane, choose the team you want to archive, and at the bottom of the row, click on **...** to open the options menu.

3. In the menu, click on **Archive team**:

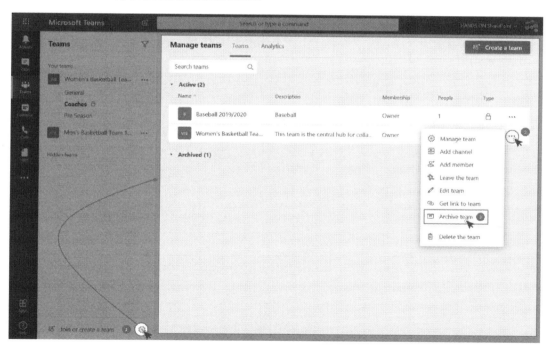

Figure 5.19: Archiving a team

4. Choose whether you want to make the SharePoint site collection associated with the team read-only:

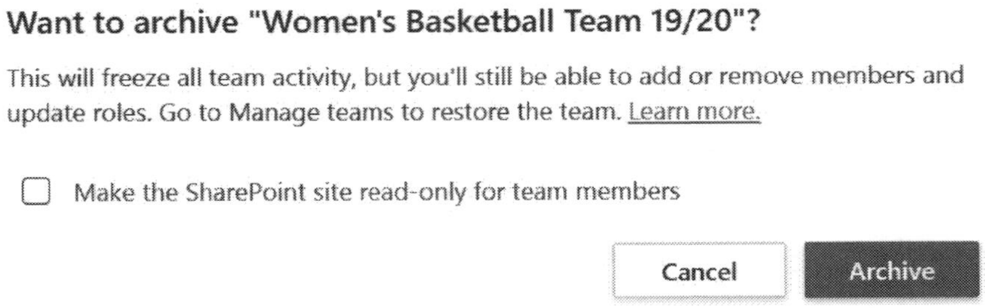

Want to archive "Women's Basketball Team 19/20"?

This will freeze all team activity, but you'll still be able to add or remove members and update roles. Go to Manage teams to restore the team. Learn more.

☐ Make the SharePoint site read-only for team members

Cancel   Archive

Figure 5.20: Archive confirmation

5. Click on **Archive**.

After archiving a team, if you decide that it's necessary to make it active again, you can do so.

An archived team can still be accessed; however, it will display a message at the top informing the user that the team cannot be modified, as in the following screenshot:

This team was archived, so you can't make any changes.

Figure 5.21: An archived team message

> **Restoring a team scenario—Geno the basketball coach**
>
> Geno has archived the team for the current season but he had forgotten about the runner-up celebration. To notify all the team members that contributed to the season's success, Geno has restored the team again and posted an announcement to the general channel with information about the celebration.

To restore an archived team, do the following:

1. In the **Manage teams** panel in Microsoft Teams, click on the cog icon at the bottom of the left pane.

2. Expand the **Archived** pane, choose the team you want to restore, and at the bottom of the row, click on ... to open the options menu.

3. From the menu, click on **Restore team**.

4. A popup will open while the team is being restored and after a few seconds, it's ready to be used again.

5. If a team is no longer needed, you can delete it permanently, along with all the assets associated with it. Before deleting a team, you should be aware that its mailbox and calendar in Exchange are also deleted, along with the SharePoint site collection and all the files in it.

> **Deleting a team scenario—Mary the consultant**
>
> Mary is a consultant and, over the last few months, has been working on a project for a software company. To manage all the requirements and share them with coworkers and the software company during the project, Mary has created a private team in Microsoft Teams. After delivering the project successfully, the software company requested that Mary delete all the sensitive information from the team. Since Mary was the team owner, she went ahead and deleted the entire team, removing any information related to the software company from the consulting tenant.

To delete a team, do the following:

1. In the **Manage teams** panel in Microsoft Teams, click on the cog icon at the bottom of the left pane.

2. Expand the **Active** pane, choose the team you want to archive and at the bottom of the row, click on ... to open the options menu.

3. At the bottom of the menu, click on **Delete the team**:

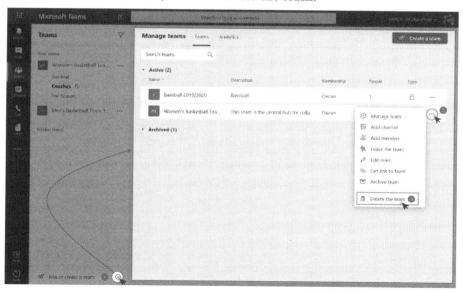

Figure 5.22: Deleting a team

4. Tick the checkbox that acknowledges that you understand that everything will be deleted:

Figure 5.23: Delete confirmation

5. Click on **Delete team**.

> **Important note**
>
> A deleted team can be recovered by the team owner or the Microsoft Teams admin within the 30 days after deletion. The 30 days are inherited by the soft delete period from Office 365 groups. After 30 days, the team and all the content are permanently deleted.

Restoring a deleted team is not as straightforward as restoring an archived team. To get back a team within the 30 days after deletion, do the following:

1. Open the **Microsoft 365 admin center**: `https://admin.microsoft.com`

2. In the left-hand side pane, click on **Groups** and then **Deleted groups**.

3. Select the group that you want to restore.

4. Click **Restore group**:

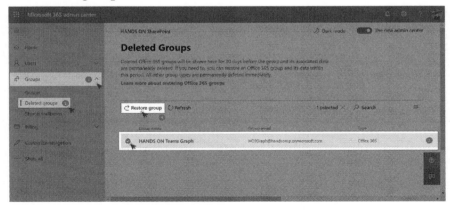

Figure 5.24: Restoring a group

5. Wait for the confirmation message that will appear on the right side. The group and all the team assets can take up to 24 hours to restore, after which they will appear in Teams.

> **Note**
> Deleting a team does not delete the team recordings in Microsoft Stream.

Deleting channels

Like teams, channels can also be deleted when they are no longer needed. However, the content removed from a team is different between standard and private channels. When a standard channel is deleted, only the conversations are removed from the tenant; the files remain in the SharePoint document library.

When a private channel is removed, all the chats and files are removed with it and the SharePoint site collection is also removed. Like teams, channels can also be recovered within 30 days of being deleted. As a team owner, if you want to recover a deleted channel, do the following:

1. Click on ... next to the name of the team.

2. In the options menu, click on **Manage team**.

3. In the stage area, click on the **Channels** tab and expand the **Deleted** section.

4. Click on the **Restore** button, as in the following screenshot:

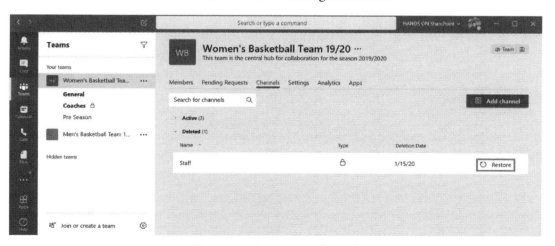

Figure 5.25: Restoring a channel

5. The recovery of deleted channels can take up to 24 hours and is available for standard and private channels.

Now that we have understood team creation governance, we will have to organize these different teams and channels. Let's see how to do so in the next section.

Organizing teams and channels

Over time, while working with Microsoft Teams, you will end up with dozens of teams and channels in your account. Not all of them will have the same importance and you will want to be able to access the ones that are more relevant to you first.

To help you organize your teams and channels, Microsoft Teams offers the option of pinning your most relevant channels, which are the ones displayed at the top of your teams list, inside a **Pinned** group:

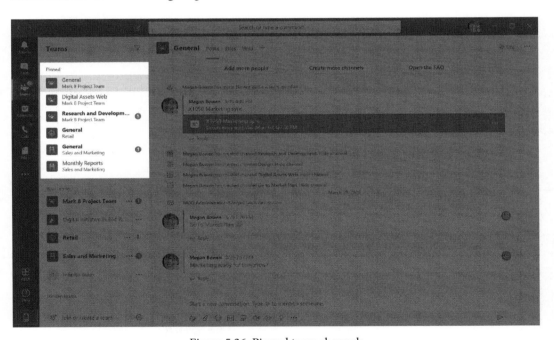

Figure 5.26: Pinned team channels

To make use of the pinning feature, do the following:

1. Click on **…** next to the channel name to open the options menu.

2. Click on **Pin**:

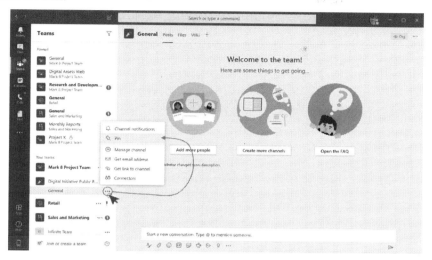

Figure 5.27: Pinning a channel

3. The channel added to the **Pinned** group is identified by the team logo, channel name, and team name. By default, a new pinned channel is added to the bottom of the list, but you can manually sort them by clicking on the pinned channel and, without releasing, dragging it to the desired position:

Figure 5.28: Sorting a pinned channel by dragging it to the desired position

> **Note**
>
> The sorting feature using drag and drop is valid for all **Teams, Pinned, Your Teams**, and **Hidden Teams** groups.

Pinning a channel is available to organization members and guest users and works with standard and private channels

Pinned channels can also be unpinned to be removed from the top of the list. To remove a channel from the **Pinned** group, do the following:

1. Click on **...** next to the channel name to open the options menu.

2. Click on **Unpin**:

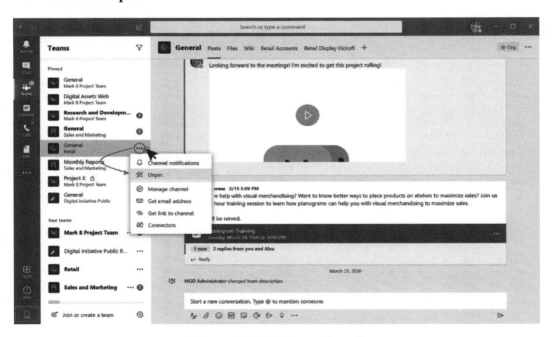

Figure 5.29: Unpinning a channel

It's not uncommon to belong to a team that is not relevant to you, so to stay organized and keep your teams list clean, you can hide all the teams that you typically don't use.

A hidden team is added to the **Hidden Teams** group by doing the following:

1. Click on **...** next to the team name to open the options menu.

2. Click on **Hide**:

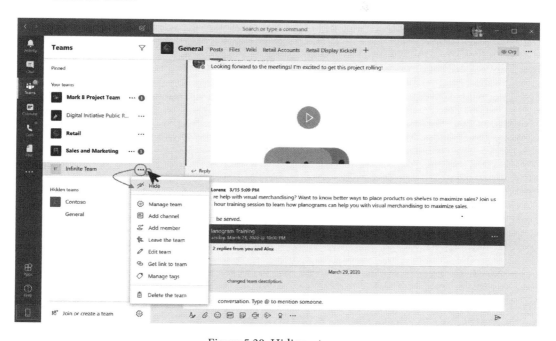

Figure 5.30: Hiding a team

Using the features described in this section, you will be able to keep your teams organized, which will help you to stay focused on the locations where your work needs to be done.

Understanding team and channel limits

Microsoft Teams was designed to support large organizations; however, it is not unlimited and there are some boundaries in all the features we have seen in this chapter. When planning a new environment, you should always do so keeping the boundaries of each feature of Microsoft Teams in mind. By knowing them and planning the structure of the tenant ahead of time, you will avoid encountering the limits of the platform.

The following table shows the platform limits for teams and channels:

Feature	Limit
Teams created per user	250
Maximum number of teams per user	1,000
Maximum number of members in a team	10,000
Organization-wide teams limit per tenant	5
Maximum number of members in an organization-wide team	10,000
Maximum number of teams per tenant	500,000
Maximum number of standard channels per team (deleted channels included)	200
Maximum number of private channels per team (deleted channels included)	30

Keep the team and channel limits in mind before you start implementing a new team. By knowing them and planning the structure of the tenant ahead of time, you will avoid encountering the limits of the platform.

Summary

In this chapter, you have learned the functionalities associated with the main core features of Microsoft Teams. You saw examples of scenarios that will help you to decide when to use standard or private teams and channels.

You have also been introduced to the limits of the platform for teams, channels, and the number of users. By being aware of these limits, you will be able to plan and deploy Microsoft Teams effectively in large organizations.

In the following chapter, we will look at how you can extend Microsoft Teams functionalities to adapt them to your business needs using apps.

6
Extending Microsoft Teams Using Apps

Microsoft Teams is more than a communication platform, and its features are not limited to chat and meetings.

Microsoft Teams can be used to handle daily communication with colleagues, almost replacing internal emails. On the other hand, it can be extended with apps to support business logic that is not included by default in the application, removing the necessity to use third-party tools or bring those tools into the Microsoft Teams context.

This chapter introduces Microsoft Teams apps and explains how to get started with the app store, using available apps as examples.

In the following pages, you will find information about these main topics:

- Understanding apps in Microsoft Teams
- Installing apps on Microsoft Teams
- Getting familiar with Microsoft Teams app types
- Managing personal apps
- Uninstalling apps from Microsoft Teams

Understanding apps in Microsoft Teams

One of the weapons of Microsoft Teams is the apps you can add to it to enhance its features and make the user experience of the application better.

Apps open a wide variety of possibilities and configurations that allow you to tailor Microsoft Teams exactly according to your needs and following your own procedures and workflows.

Using apps, you will be able to bring to Microsoft Teams information and data that is stored in third-party applications. This is important in the modern workplace environment because it allows the user to continue in the same environment without the need to switch between applications.

According to the study *The total economic impact of Microsoft Teams* from *April 2019*, *"Information workers save 15 minutes per day and firstline workers 5 minutes per day by having features and information sources available within Teams, rather than switching between apps. Time savings cover the mechanics of switching and cognitive re-engagement. The total savings over three years is nearly $4.8 million."*

The app experience on Teams is no different than the experience we all know in our phones and in our computers. Teams has its own application store where users can go and look for apps that suit their needs. Apps are divided into five different categories that we will look at in detail:

- **Personal apps**: These give you a personal view of your work and can be installed and configured by you according to your needs.
- **Bots**: A bot brings you information from other apps using natural language. You can query the bot and it will send you the right information
- **Tabs**: You can add the applications you need as tabs in the context of channels and one-to-one or group chats
- **Connectors**: Connectors will post notifications from other services to your channels.
- **Messaging**: Messaging apps include information in a card format from external services and post it to group, team, or one-to-one chats.

These five types of app allow you to bring information from third-party systems into meetings, chats, and calls with just a few clicks without ever leaving the Microsoft Teams ecosystem. An app can include support for one or more categories. This means it will have different behaviors when installed, which you can take advantage of and reuse in different scenarios. Now that we know what Microsoft Teams apps are, let's look at how to install them in the next section.

Installing apps on Microsoft Teams

Any user of Microsoft Teams (with the exception of guests) is able to install apps. You just need to open the app store and select the desired app, as shown in the following steps:

1. To open the app store in Microsoft Teams, click on the **Apps** icon in the sidebar.

2. The app store will open in the stage area, as shown in the following screenshot:

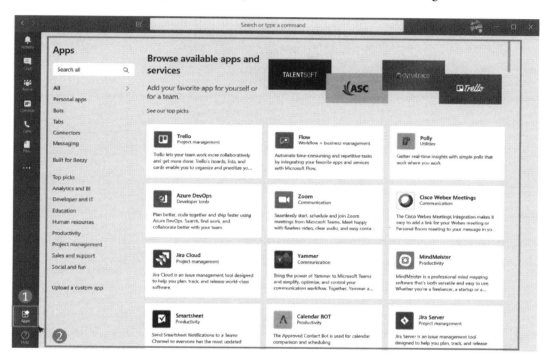

Figure 6.1: Microsoft Teams app store

3. By default, the store opens with the unfiltered list of all the available apps for your region, but the search and the vertical menu with the categories and types can be used to refine it.

4. Select the app you want to install and click on it.

5. A pop-up window like the one in the following screenshot will open, and from it you will be able to get a preview of the app running on Microsoft Teams, a description of the features, and access to privacy and permissions:

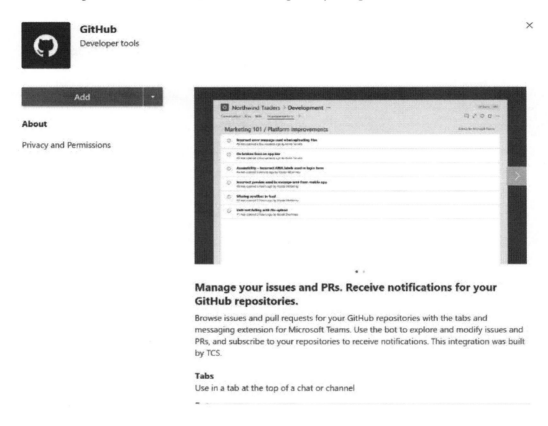

Figure 6.2: Adding a new app

6. Click on **Add** to install the app.

Remember, depending of the app type, the **Add** button might assume different layouts with different options. The following screenshots show the possible variants:

Figure 6.3: Variations on the Add button

(a) **Add** means that the app will become available globally.

(b) **Add to a team** means that the app will be installed in a team. When the button just shows this option, it means the app cannot be used in any other context and you will not be able to use it as a personal app.

(c) **Add to a chat** means that the app can be installed and added to a group chat or to a one-to-one chat.

(d) **Open** isn't shown in the image. This option means that the app is already installed in your tenant and is ready to use.

Now that we have installed our apps, let's explore and implement the different types of apps in the next section.

Getting familiar with Microsoft Teams app types

This section will help you to understand each of the five app types by beginning with scenarios and with sample apps selected from the store.

The scenarios are described with configuration instructions. Please note that the options might be different depending on the app you will be using in your environment.

The examples are the typical scenarios that will boost your productivity when using Microsoft Teams. By using the apps on Microsoft Teams, you will be able to do most of your tasks without losing focus and wasting time switching between applications. So, let's get right to it.

Personal apps

Let's begin with our first scenario:

> **João, the book writer**
>
> João is writing a book about Microsoft Teams and is using Microsoft Planner to help with the deadlines and the requests made by the editor. Since João is writing about Microsoft Teams and using it intensively, he pinned Microsoft Planner as a personal app; this way, all the remaining tasks for the book are just one click away.

Microsoft Planner is pre-installed on Microsoft Teams, and to start using it as a personal app, all you have to do is this:

1. Click on the three dots on the app menu to expand the submenu with all the personal apps available for you.

2. Click on Microsoft Planner. Since it is part of your Office 365 subscription, you don't need to provide authentication. Planner will immediately display your tasks, as shown in the following screenshot:

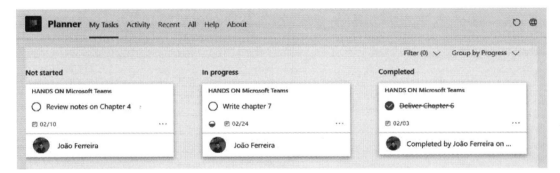

Figure 6.4: Personal app

Bots

We will now take a look at our second scenario:

> **John, the developer**
>
> John is a developer working on an open source project available on GitHub. John and the other project members are communicating through Microsoft Teams and are using the GitHub app to easily get an overview of all the open issues and to assign them to the right person.

To install the GitHub app on Microsoft Teams, do the following:

1. Open the Teams app store.

2. On the vertical menu, click on **Bots**.

3. Search for `GitHub` and click on it.

4. Click on **Add to team**.

5. Look for the channel where you want to add it.

6. Set up the connection to GitHub. This is required to grant permissions to get information from the GitHub repositories.

The interaction with bots is done through the chat, and you will be able to use natural language to question the application, which will reply to you using the intelligent mechanism it was built with.

Since bots and users are posting messages in the same chats, Microsoft Teams identifies bot messages with a hexagonal profile picture instead of using a round one, which is reserved for real users.

To interact with a bot, all you have to do is mention it in the chat window and then type the keywords that the bot will use to query the system. A mention on Microsoft Teams starts with @ followed by the name of the bot or the person.

If you are not sure of what you can do with the bot, check the **What can I do?** section shown in the following screenshot. It will show an overview of the commands that the bot understands. This option becomes available when you mention a bot, and it is demonstrated in the following screenshot. You can also see the hexagonal profile picture of the bot:

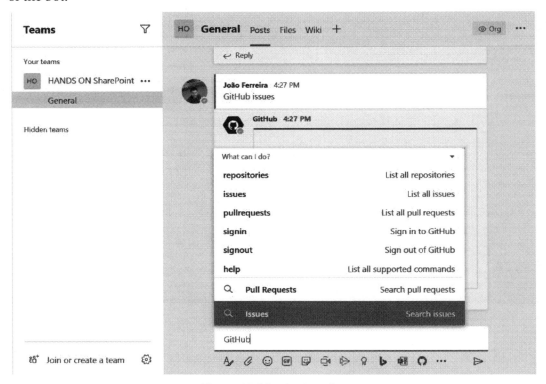

Figure 6.5: Mentioning a bot

If the bot doesn't know the answer to one of your questions, it will inform you so you can use alternative methods to find the information you are looking for:

Figure 6.6: Interaction with a bot

Successful replies are always made in the thread where the question was asked, and the results are displayed in a card format.

If you perform an action in the card that triggers a new question to the bot, it will reply in the same thread, keeping all the information related to the interaction aggregated in one location.

The following screenshot shows a thread conversation between a user and a bot. The user asked for the issues and, when they clicked on one of them, it triggered a new question to the bot, which replied with the issue details:

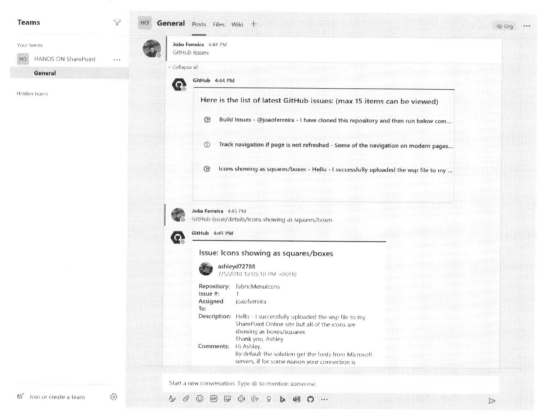

Figure 6.7: Bot conversation

Tabs

We now move on to our third scenario to understand how tabs are used:

> **Francis, the customer success manager**
>
> Francis is the customer success manager in an IT company and is responsible for keeping the customers happy. Francis' team has members all around the world, and to keep everyone in sync they are using Microsoft Teams.
>
> Customers are reporting issues and requesting support using Zendesk, a customer service tool, which integrates with Microsoft Teams. To keep the information centralized and to get an immediate overview of all the requests, Francis added Zendesk for Microsoft Teams to a tab on the customer success team; this way, she can monitor the status of the tickets.

To add Zendesk as a tab on Microsoft Teams, do the following:

1. Open the Teams app store.

2. On the vertical menu, click on **Tabs**.

3. Search for **Zendesk** and click on it.

4. Search for the channel where you want to add the tab and click on **Setup**.

5. Authenticate and select the ticket view you want to display on the tab:

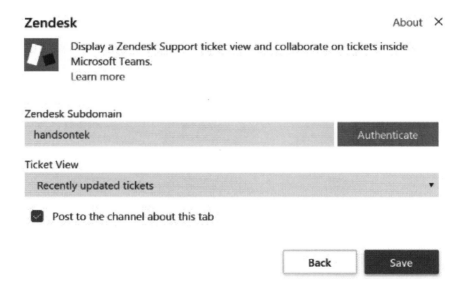

Figure 6.8: Tab configuration

6. Click **Save**.

7. A new tab is created in the channel with the name of the view, and you will be able to interact with the support system. If you need to create more tabs to display other views, repeat the entire process:

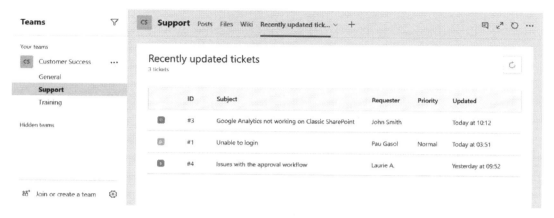

Figure 6.9: Tab

Tabs allow you to modify the configurations after being added to the team. This way, if you make a mistake or if you simply want to change what is being displayed, you can modify it without deleting the tab and go through the installation process again.

Tabs can only be modified by Team owners. To do this, follow these steps:

1. Open the tab you want to modify.

2. Next to the tab name, click on the down arrow.

3. Click on **Settings**. This menu also has the option to rename or remove a tab:

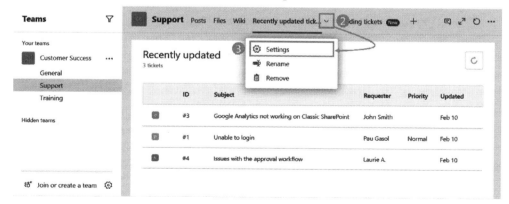

Figure 6.10: Tab settings

4. A popup will open with the configurations for the tab. Note that the configuration options will be different in most of the tabs you have installed on Microsoft Teams.

Connectors

In this scenario, we will see how connectors are useful.

> **Susan, the marketing manager**
>
> Susan is the marketing manager of a Formula E racing team and is responsible for collecting everything Formula E-related that is posted by the press. To collect the news, Susan is using the RSS connector configured to get news from the main sites that cover the sport. Every time one of them publishes a new article, it also gets published on Susan's media channel on Microsoft Teams.

To add the RSS or any other connector available in the store to one of your teams, do the following:

1. Open the Teams app store.

2. On the vertical menu, click on **Connectors**.

3. Search for **RSS** and click on the application.

4. In the pop-up window, click on **Add to a team**:

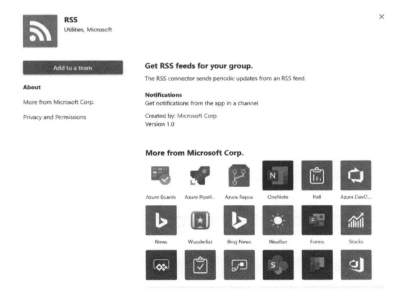

Figure 6.11: Adding a connector

5. Select the team and the channel where you want to set up the connector.

6. Click on **Set up connector**.

7. Enter a name for the RSS connection.

8. Enter the RSS feed URL.

9. Choose the digest frequency.

10. Click on **Save**:

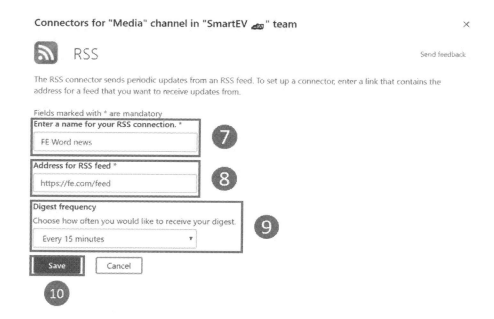

Figure 6.12: Setting up a connector

Messages posted by the connector are added in a card format, and each connector has its own profile picture. Profile pictures used by the connectors have a hexagonal format to help users distinguish them from real users' profiles, which are displayed with a circular picture:

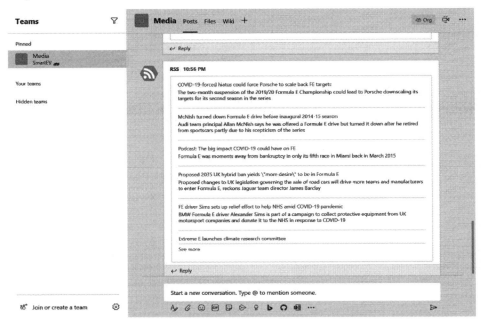

Figure 6.13: Connector message

Connectors added to channels can be modified or removed according to a user's needs. To modify a running connector from a channel, do the following:

1.   Open the channel where you want to modify the connector.

2.   Click on the three dots next to the name of the channel or in the top-right corner to open the context menu.

3.   In the context menu, click on **Connectors**.

4.   A popup will open showing the list of all connectors. The ones applied to the team are in the **Connectors for your team** section:

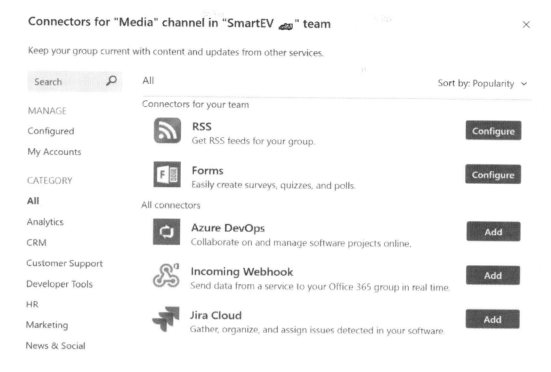

Figure 6.14: Managing channel connectors

5. Click on the **Configure** button.

6. Reconfigure the connector and click on **Save**.

Messaging extensions

In this last scenario, we will try to understand when we can use messaging extensions.

> **Geno, the basketball coach**
>
> Geno is a basketball coach planning to schedule a party to celebrate the success of the season, but he is unsure about the date. Throughout the season, Geno used Microsoft Teams to communicate with the athletes and staff members, so he will use it one more time to do a poll regarding the celebration date. Geno will use a messaging app called Microsoft Forms, an extension of the platform with the same name that is included in Office 365. Using this, he will be able to post the poll to the General channel, and everybody will be able to vote and see the results.

To add Microsoft Forms or any other messaging app, do the following:

1. Open the Teams app store.

2. On the vertical menu, click on **Messaging**.

3. In the search box, type Forms.

4. In the app listing, click on **Forms**.

5. In the pop-up window, click on the arrow to open the dropdown and then click on **Add**:

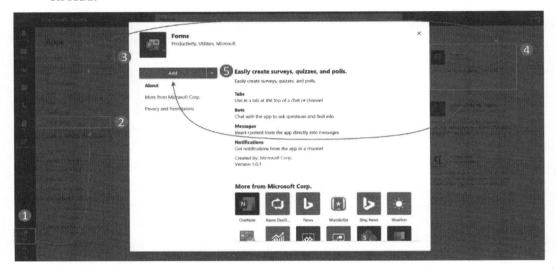

Figure 6.15: Adding a messaging extension

Now that you have the app installed, it's time to use it. Messaging apps, once installed, become available to all the users, and you can find them next to the textbox used to type messages. To create a new form, do the following:

1. Open the channel or the chat where you want to post the form.

2. Under the textbox, click on the Forms icon.

3. In the popup, type the question for the poll and add the options.

4. Click on **Next**:

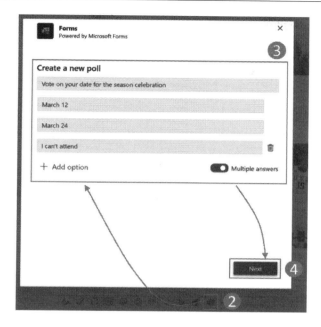

Figure 6.16: Composing the message using the extension

5. If the preview looks as you expect, click on **Send**.

6. The form and the poll result are added to the channels and the chat window so anyone can vote and see the results:

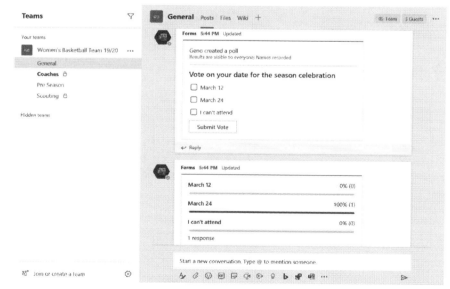

Figure 6.17: Message posted using the extension

Now that we have had a look at all the different types of Microsoft Apps, in our next section, we will see how to manage our personal apps in a better way.

Managing personal apps

Personal apps were designed to boost your productivity, and they will always display content that is tailored to you. Personal apps can be launched from the vertical menu, and they can be configured by you or by the admin to better suit your needs.

The amount of space on the app bar is limited, and if there is no space to display all your apps, they will be shown in a submenu that is revealed when you click on the three dots, as shown in the following screenshot:

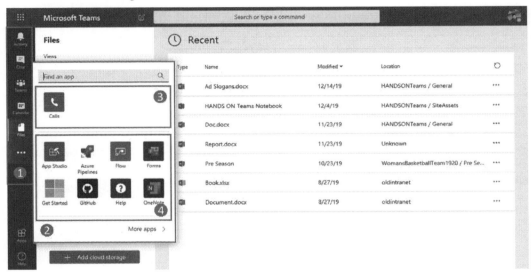

Figure 6.18: Personal apps

Let's take a look at what each of these mean:

1. The app bar showing the pinned apps and the **...** to open the **More apps** menu.
2. All the personal apps that are not visible in the app bar are shown in this menu.

3. A group with all the pinned apps that are not displayed in the app bar due to the lack of space.

4. A group of all the unpinned personal apps that you have available.

> **Pro tip**
>
> Personal apps can be displayed with two different icons. The apps that are not pinned to the menu display a colored icon inside the submenu, while pinned apps are displayed with a white icon typically showing the outline of the icon.

Open personal apps can be identified in the app bar by the selected layout; however, it is different for pinned and unpinned apps:

Figure 6.19: Pinned app versus an unpinned app

5. Open **pinned** apps are displayed in its own position in the menu bar and in regular font.

6. Open **unpinned** apps are displayed at the bottom of the menu bar and in italic font.

By default, Microsoft Teams displays five apps in the app bar (**Activity**, **Chat**, **Teams**, **Calendar**, and **Files**), but this can be changed by you as an end user or by the Microsoft Teams administrator.

Personalizing the app bar as an end user

To remove personal apps from the app bar, including the default ones, you need to right-click the app name and then select the **Unpin** option. Unpinned apps will be displayed in the submenu, and they can be pinned at any given time.

To pin personal apps to the app bar, you need to right-click the app in the submenu and then select the **Pin** option:

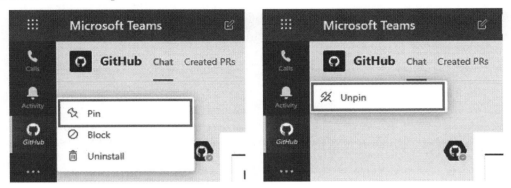

Figure 6.20: Pinning/unpinning an app

Pinned apps are displayed in the order they were pinned, but if you are using the client version of Microsoft Teams for desktop, you will be able to change the order by dragging them to the desired position:

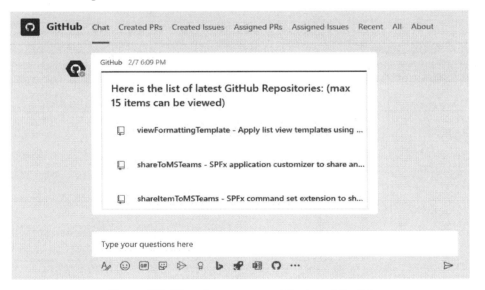

Figure 6.21: Pinned apps appear at the top of the list

Note
If the options to customize the app bar are not available, you should contact your Microsoft Teams administrator as this option can be enabled/disabled globally.

Personalizing the app bar as an administrator

A Microsoft Teams administrator can personalize the default look of the personal app for all the users in the organization through the user of custom policies. This allows the admin to set up different layouts for the app bar that can then be applied to users individually according to their roles.

If you have administrator permissions and want to create a new company layout for the app bar, do the following:

1. Open **Microsoft Teams admin center**: `https://admin.teams.microsoft.com/`

2. From the vertical menu, click on **Teams apps** and then **Setup policies**.

3. Click on **Add** to create a new policy:

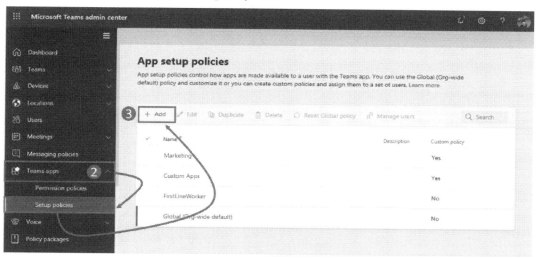

Figure 6.22: Creating a new app setup policy

4. Provide a name and a description for your new policy.

5. Choose whether you will allow your users to upload their own custom apps. Custom apps are covered in *Chapter 7, Extending Microsoft Teams Using Custom Apps and Microsoft 365.*

6. Choose whether you will allow your users to pin/unpin their own apps. By disabling this option, you will remove the option to customize the personal app bar.

7. Click on **Add apps** to add the new apps.

8. Sort or remove existing apps. By default, any new policy will start with the five default apps from Microsoft Teams.

9. Click **Save**:

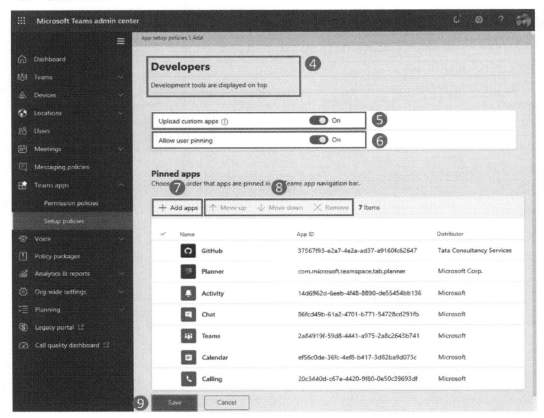

Figure 6.23: Defining the app setup policy with a custom personal app bar

New policies only take effect when assigned to one or multiple users. To assign your newly created policy, do the following:

1. From the vertical menu, click on **Users**.

2. Select the user to whom you want to apply the policy and click **Edit settings**.

3. Select the users you want to apply the new policy to.

4. Click on **Edit settings**.

5. On the **App Setup Policy** screen, select your newly created policy.

6. Click **Save**. New policies can take up to 24 hours to be applied to users.

Pro tip

You can assign policies to one or more people in your organization. However, it's recommended that you only do 20 people at a time. If you need to assign to more than 20 users, you can do so in batches or use PowerShell.

Managing the app installation as an administrator

By default, any app can be installed in Microsoft Teams. However, this setting can be modified by the global administrator by modifying or creating app permission policies.

App permission polices divide the apps into three categories:

- Microsoft apps: Any app published by Microsoft

- Third-party apps: Apps published on the Microsoft Teams app store by other vendors

- Tenant apps: Custom apps uploaded to Microsoft Teams

To restrict the use of apps in any one of these categories, do the following:

1. Open **Microsoft Teams admin center**: `https://admin.teams.microsoft.com/`

2. From the vertical menu, click on **Teams Apps** and then **Permission Policies**.

3. Click on **Add** to create a new policy, or click on **Global (Org-wide default)** if you want to modify the default settings of Microsoft Teams.

4. Choose the setting for the app categories. Each one has four options that you can choose from:

   (a) **Allow all apps**: Users can install and use any app.

   (b) **Allow specific apps and block others**: Allow specific apps you want to allow and all the other ones will be blocked.

   (c) **Block specific apps and allow others**: Add which apps you want to block and all the other ones will be allowed.

   (d) **Block all apps**: Users are unable to install apps.

5. Configure your policy according to your needs and click **Save**.

6. Options (b) and (c) will require you to manually select the apps you want to block or allow, respectively. The following screenshot shows a custom app policy for marketing members that allows all Microsoft apps, just allows the installation of four apps from the store, and blocks the installation of custom apps:

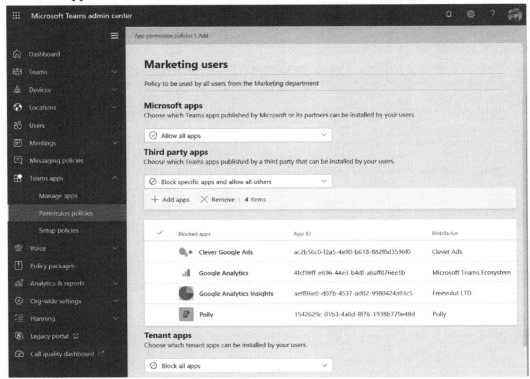

Figure 6.24: App permission policies

After creating a new policy, you need to apply it to those users who will be affected by it. To do this, do the following:

1. In **Microsoft Teams admin center**, click on **Users**.

2. Select the users to whom you want to apply the policy.

3. Click on **Edit settings**.

4. In the **App permission policy**, select the policy you want to apply.

5. Click on **Apply**:

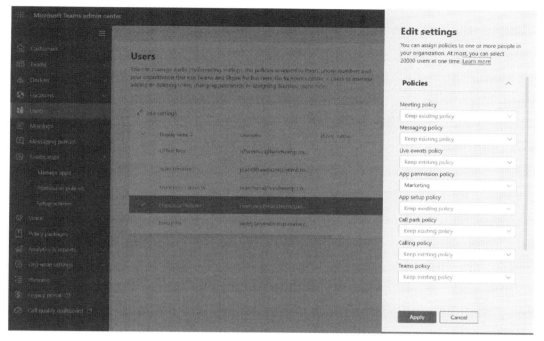

Figure 6.25: Assigning an app permission policy to a user

By using the app permission policy, you will get control over the apps that specific groups of users can install in Teams. Use it carefully! Excessive restrictions can make your users look for solutions outside the Microsoft ecosystem, putting your data at risk.

Managing apps as an administrator

As an administrator, you can control what apps are available to users in your Microsoft Teams app store. This can be done through policies, as we saw in the previous section, or can be blocked globally in the admin center.

To block or allow applications in your organization, do the following:

1. Open **Microsoft Teams admin center:** `https://admin.teams.microsoft.com/`

2. From the vertical menu, click on **Teams Apps** and then **Manage apps**.

3. Look for the app you want to control.

4. Select the app and, from the top bar, click on **Allow** or **Block**:

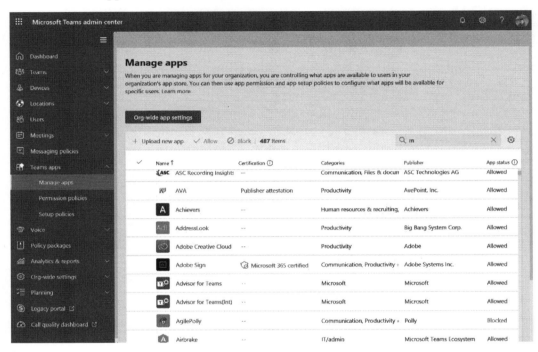

Figure 6.26: Manage apps

In the **Manage apps** table, you will find all the information you need about the application to help you decide whether to allow or block it, and the following list describes what you can find in each column:

- **Name**: The name of the app. When you click on it, it shows the details of the app, including the current version published in the store and the App ID:

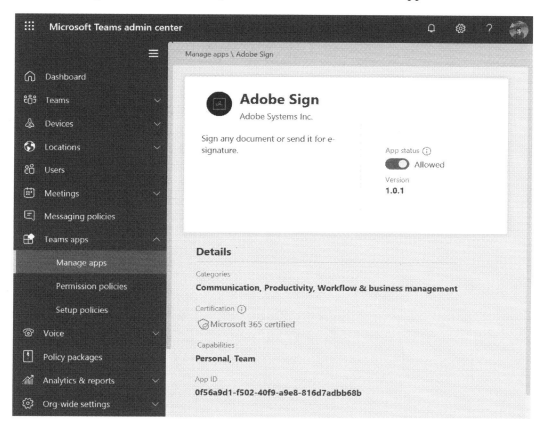

Figure 6.27: App details

- **Certification**: In this field, you will see the level of certification. This means that the publisher or Microsoft have verified the application and the results of the certification are publicly available. In this field, you can find the values **Publish Attestation**, **Microsoft 365 certified**, or it can be empty. When you click on one of the values, it will open the Microsoft portal, showing all the information about data handling, security, and compliance, helping you to decide whether to keep the app in the tenant:

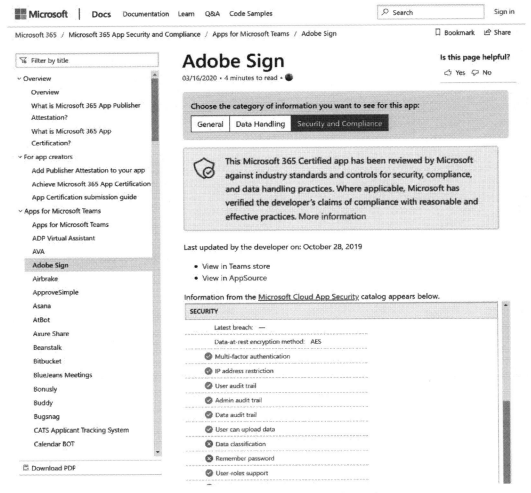

Figure 6.28: App certification detail portal

- **Categories**: A list of categories where the app is included.

- **Publisher**: The name of the publisher.

- **App status**: This contains more information about the app's status at the organizational level. **Allowed** means that the app is available for users in your organization. **Blocked** means that the app isn't available for users in your organization.

- **Custom App**: Indicates whether the app was uploaded manually to the tenant or if it is available in the store. To find out more about custom apps, refer to *Chapter 7, Extend Microsoft Teams Using Custom Apps and Microsoft 365*.

In the **Manage apps** section, you will be able to carefully review all the apps available in the store and decide to allow or block them, keeping your Microsoft Teams tenant and data secure.

Uninstalling apps from Microsoft Teams

On Microsoft Teams, you will find different ways of uninstalling an app depending on its type. In this section, all the removal processes are detailed, so you can remove apps if you are no longer using them.

Apps that are installed in a team need to be uninstalled from the team directly. This process applies to tabs, connectors, bots, and messaging. To remove one these apps, do the following:

1. Open the team where the app is installed.

2. Click on the **...** next to the name of the team to open the context menu.

3. In the context menu, click on **Manage team**.

4. Click on the **Apps** tab.

5. Look for the app in the list and click on the trash can icon:

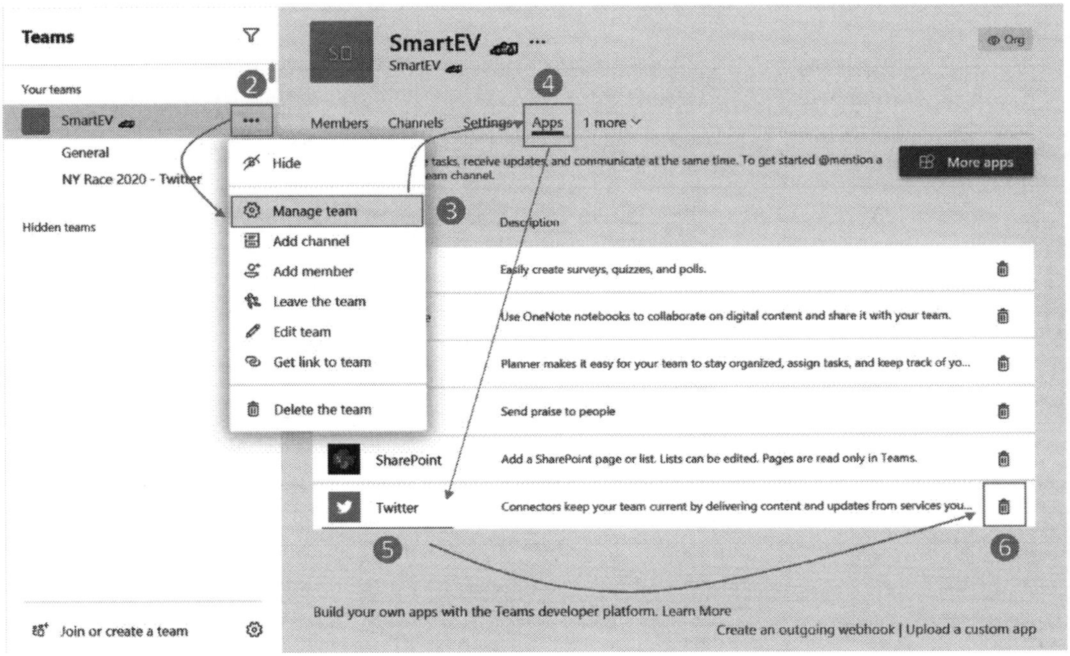

Figure 6.29: Uninstalling an app from a team

6. In the confirmation popup, click on **Uninstall**.

Personal apps need to be uninstalled by you directly from the app bar where the app is accessible from. To do this, perform the following steps:

1. Locate the app you want to remove and right-click on it.

2. In the context menu, click on **Uninstall**:

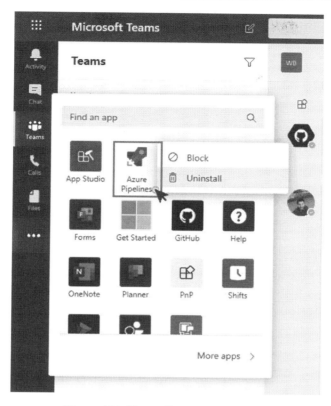

Figure 6.30: Uninstalling a personal app

3. In the confirmation popup, click on **Uninstall** and, after a few seconds, the app will be removed.

> **Note**
> You can only uninstall apps that were installed by you; default apps cannot be removed.

Summary

In this chapter, you have learned what Microsoft Teams apps are and how to use them in different scenarios. You have also learned how to extend Teams using the app store to create crafted experiences with the customization of the applications available to users.

In the next chapter, you will learn how Microsoft Teams can be further customized with apps from the Microsoft ecosystem that you might already be using, such as Power Apps, Power Automate, and SharePoint.

7
Extend Microsoft Teams Using Custom Apps and Microsoft 365

Microsoft Teams can be extended using apps from app store as we have seen in the previous chapter but it can be also extended with custom apps built for your business specifically. In this section of the book, you will learn how custom apps can be enabled on your tenant and how you can use other tools from the Microsoft 365 ecosystem to extend the default functionalities.

If you are using SharePoint, Power Apps, or Power Automate, in this chapter you will learn how to integrate these three platforms with Microsoft Teams.

In the following pages, you will find information about these main topics:

- Working with custom apps
- Installing custom apps
- Blocking Microsoft Teams apps

- Extending Microsoft Teams using SharePoint
- Extending Microsoft Teams using PowerAutomate
- Extending Microsoft Teams using PowerApps

Working with custom apps

Organizations are all different and have their own rules and internal processes. However, even though the Microsoft Teams store provides an awesome way of extending the platform, it will not be able to cover all the requirements of the different organizations.

To overcome this problem, Microsoft Teams allows you to upload custom apps built by developers for your organization. This way, you will be able to extend the platform according to your specifications.

Enabling custom apps

Custom apps must be enabled by the administrator and in this section, we will see how it can be done:

1. Start by opening the **Microsoft Teams admin center** at `https://admin.teams.microsoft.com`.

2. On the vertical menu, expand **Teams apps** and then click on **Manage apps.**

3. Click on the **Org-wide app settings** button:

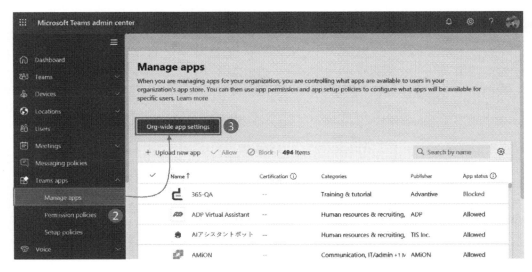

Figure 7.1: Org-wide settings

4. Toggle the option **Allow interaction with custom apps** to **On**. This way, you can allow your users to upload custom apps that are not available in the store:

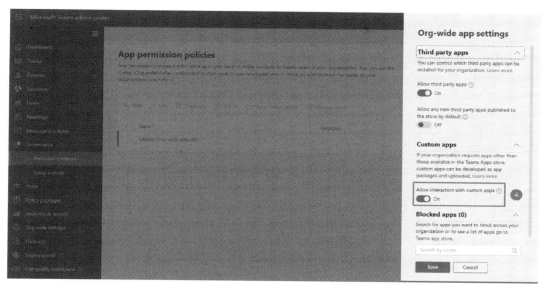

Figure 7.2: Enabling interaction with custom apps

5. Click **Save**.

As an administrator, you should be careful with the rollout of custom apps into Microsoft Teams. You should only install apps from trusted sources and you should plan who will be able to install this type of app. Even though custom apps get enabled globally in the org-wide settings, you can restrict who will be able to upload them through the use of setup policies, which is what we will see in the next section.

Disabling custom apps

Custom apps will be able to access information on your tenants, so it's recommended to plan which users will have the necessary permissions to install them. To restrict the installation of custom apps, you can disable this functionality on the **Global (Org-wide default)** policy – this way, each new user will not have the ability to upload custom apps. To do it, follow these steps:

1. Open the Microsoft Teams admin center.

2. On the vertical menu, expand **Teams apps** and then click on **Setup policies**.

3. Select **Global (Org-wide default)**.

4.   Click on the **Edit** button on the toolbar:

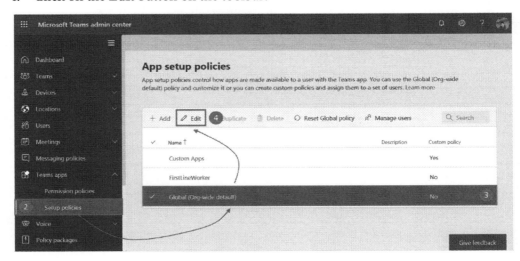

Figure 7.3: Edit App setup policies

5.   Toggle the **Upload custom apps** option to **Off**.

6.   Click **Save**, and note that modifications of these policies can take up to 24 hours to be applied:

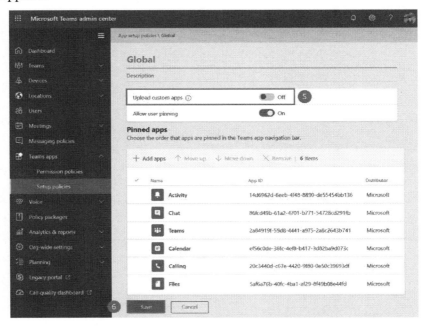

Figure 7.4: Disabling custom app upload

Uploading custom apps

Now that you have disabled the upload of custom apps globally, you need to create a new policy that allows users to upload this type of app. To create a new policy for custom apps, do the following:

1. Open the **Microsoft Teams admin center**.

2. On the vertical menu, expand **Teams apps** and then click on **Setup policies**.

3. On the toolbar, click on **Add**.

4. Provide a name and a description for your policy.

5. Toggle the **Upload custom apps** option to **On**:

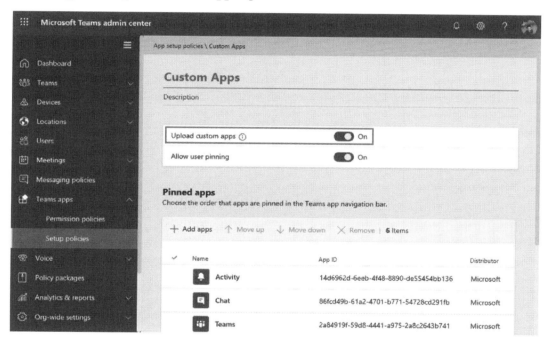

Figure 7.5: Enabling custom app upload

You now need to apply the new policy to the users who will have the power to upload custom apps. The profiles that should have access to this option are different in every organization but here are some examples you should consider:

- Administrators

- Developers

- Some team owners

To apply the custom app policy to your chosen users, do the following:

1. Open **Microsoft Teams admin center**.

2. On the vertical menu, click on **Users**.

3. Select the users that will have the power to upload these apps.

> **Note**
>
> You should not apply it to more than 20 users at a time. If you have more than 20 users, you can do this in batches or using PowerShell. PowerShell for Microsoft Teams is explained in *Chapter 10, Microsoft Teams PowerShell – a Tool for Automation*

4. Click on **Edit settings**.

5. On **App setup policy**, select your policy for **Custom Apps**.

6. Click **Apply**, remembering that custom policies can take up to 24 hours to be applied:

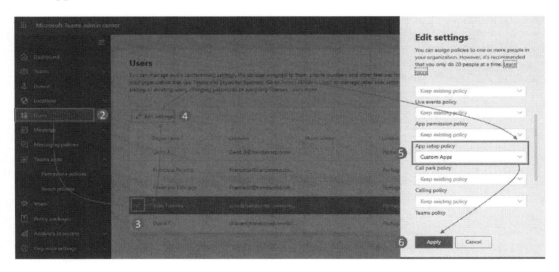

Figure 7.6: Applying a custom policy

> **Pro Tip:**
>
> When managing Microsoft Teams, you will stumble across multiple terms with reference to apps. As an admin, it's important to know all the concepts and the differences between them as they can be a bit confusing:
>
> (a) **Third-arty apps** – Third-party apps are all the apps installed by users from the app store.
>
> (b) **Custom apps or side-loading apps** – Both names are associated with apps uploaded to the tenant without using the app store.

Installing custom apps

Now that you know how to enable custom apps and how to give permissions to the right users to install them, it is time to learn how the installation process works.

> **Note:**
>
> The process described in this section uses a prebuilt custom app from Microsoft to install Microsoft Learning Pathways on Microsoft Teams. To learn more about this solution, visit `https://docs.microsoft.com/en-us/office365/customlearning/`.
>
> If you want to know more about how to build custom apps for Microsoft Teams, have a look at *Chapter 8, Build Your Own App for Microsoft Teams Using App Studio*.

If you are a user with permissions to upload custom apps, do the following:

1. Open Microsoft Teams and click on **Apps**.

2. At the bottom of the window, click on **Upload a custom app**.

3. On the menu, choose whether you want to install it globally for all the users in the tenant or just for you and your teams:

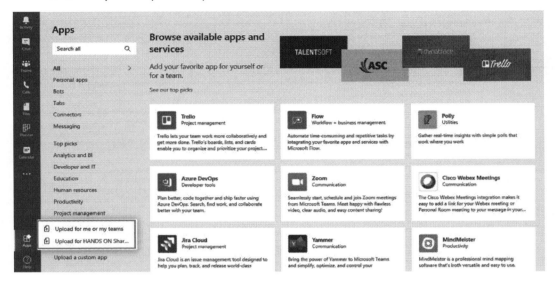

Figure 7.7: Uploading a custom app

4. Upload the ZIP file containing the app and click **Open**.

5. When you choose to install the app **for you and your teams**, a pop-up window will open and you will have to click on **Add** as shown in the following screenshot:

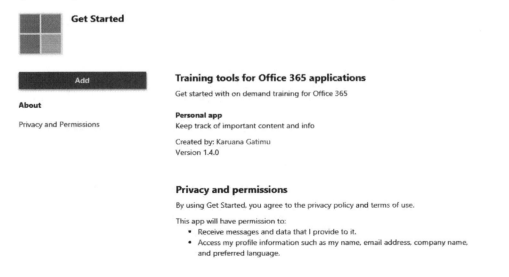

Figure 7.8: Adding a new app

6. When you choose to install the app **globally in the tenant**, after uploading the ZIP file, a new category is created in the app store's vertical menu, as shown in the following screenshot:

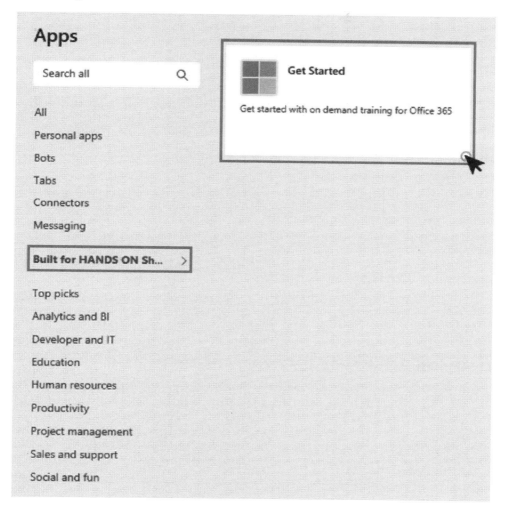

Figure 7.9: Installed custom app

7. To install the app, you need to click on it and then, on the popup, click on **Add**:

Depending on the custom app type, the **Add** button might assume different layouts with different options. The following screenshot represents the possible variants:

Figure 7.10: Add button – variations

Let's see what each of these options are:

(a) **Add**: This means that the app will become available globally.

(b) **Add to a team**: This means that the app will be installed in a team. When the button displays just this option, it means the app cannot be used in any other context and you will not be able to use it as a personal app.

(c) **Add to a chat**: This means that the app can be installed and added to a group chat or to a one-to-one chat.

(d) **Open**: This is not represented in the screenshot, but this option means that the app is already installed in your tenant and ready to be used.

Installing custom apps as an administrator

As an administrator, you will be able to install apps from the app store, as explained in the preceding section, or from the **Manage Apps** screen available in the admin center by doing the following:

1. Open the **Microsoft Teams admin center** at `https://admin.teams.microsoft.com`.

2. On the vertical menu, expand **Teams apps** and click on **Manage apps**.

3. On the toolbar, click on **Upload new app**:

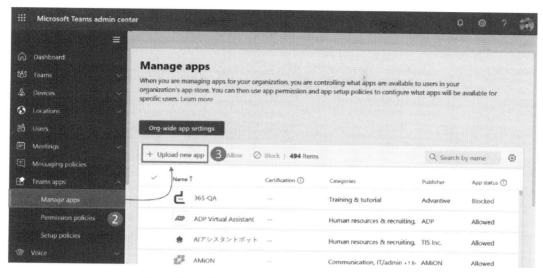

Figure 7.11: Uploading a new app as administrator

4. From the **Upload a new custom app** pop-up window, click on **Select a file**.

5. Select the ZIP file of your app and click **OK**.

6. Wait a few seconds for the confirmation message.

Apps installed from the admin center will become available to all the users in your organization.

Blocking Microsoft Teams apps

So far, we have seen how you can enable and disable the usage of Microsoft custom apps, but restricting the usage of these apps might be prejudiced against the adoption of the platform. A Microsoft Teams administrator always has the possibility to block custom apps or even apps installed from the store.

If you want to restrict the usage of apps on your tenant after being installed, do the following:

1. Start by opening the **Microsoft Teams admin center** at `https://admin.teams.microsoft.com`.

2. On the vertical menu, expand **Teams apps** and then click on **Manage apps**.

3. Click on the **Org-wide app settings** button:

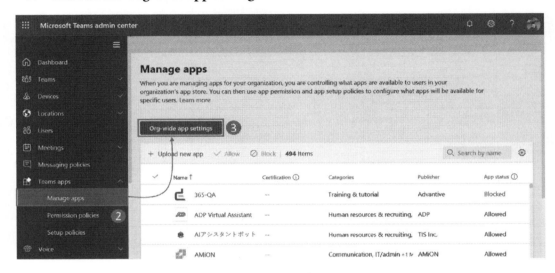

Figure 7.12: Org-wide settings

4. Scroll down on the side menu to the **Blocked apps** section.

5. Search the app you want to block by name as highlighted in the following screenshot. This search will retrieve not just the custom apps installed by you and other users, but also apps in the store that are available for you to install. Once an app is blocked by the administrator in **Org-wide app settings**, it will not be available to be used by any user in the tenant:

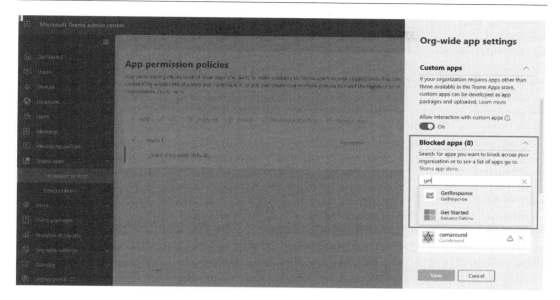

Figure 7.13: Blocked apps

Click on the name of the app you want to block and then click **Save**.

Now that you know how custom apps can be managed and installed on Microsoft Teams, as an administrator, you will be able to decide how this feature will be available to your users.

Microsoft Teams can be extended with custom apps, but also with platforms that you probably already have in-house and have been using for a long time. The next section explains how SharePoint can be used to build your own custom apps for Microsoft Teams.

Extending Microsoft Teams using SharePoint

SharePoint is one of the key components of the Microsoft Teams structure and has been around since 2001, meaning that a lot of organizations have their information systems on this platform.

The SharePoint apps described in this section come pre-installed on Microsoft Teams and are available to be used in all types of teams and channels.

Using out-of-the-box integrations

As explained in the first section of the book, each team on Microsoft Teams is built on top of a SharePoint site that is used to store information shared by the team. While SharePoint can be used just to store documents, you can also take advantage of the powerful features of the platform, such as the custom pages, news, or lists, to create complex information systems.

To bring content stored on SharePoint to Microsoft Teams, you can use the out-of-the-box apps highlighted in the following screenshot:

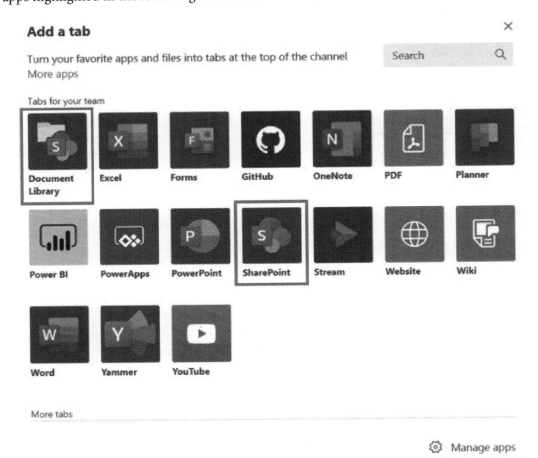

Figure 7.14: SharePoint apps

Document Library

Document Library is a tab similar to the default files tab library you get on each team. While the files tab only gets you documents from the shared documents library in the site collection, this one allows you to pick any library from any site collection. To use this app in one of your teams, do the following:

1. Add the **Document Library** tab to the channel where you want to get the documents.

2. Select the site where the document library is located either by choosing from the **Relevant sites** list or by using a SharePoint link to the site or to the library.

3. Click on **Next**:

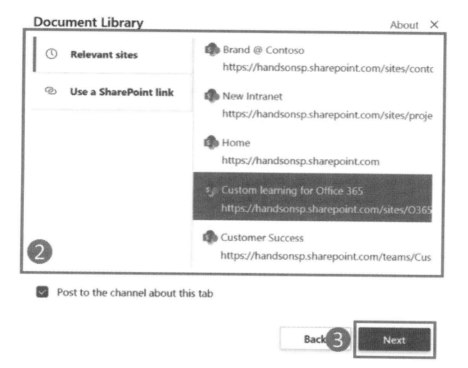

Figure 7.15: Document Library selection

4. Choose the library you want to add and click **Next**.

5. Provide a **Name** for the new tab. By default, the application suggests the name of the library.

6. Click **Save**.

The document library is a great resource when you need to bring documents from SharePoint to the Microsoft Teams context. The users will be able to perform the same actions they do on SharePoint, such as editing, uploading, renaming, and deleting files, however, the app does not give you access to custom views like the default files tab does:

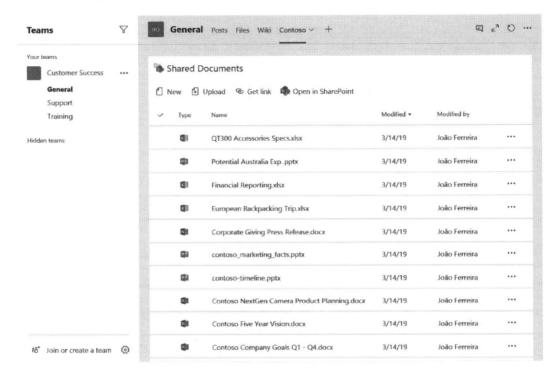

Figure 7.16: SharePoint document library

Notice that this app respects the permissions on SharePoint, which means that if the users in the team don't have access to the library selected in the app configuration, they will not see any documents.

SharePoint News

Microsoft Teams doesn't have a feature that you can use to post news and announcements for the entire team, however, you can take advantage of SharePoint to do so. SharePoint team sites include by default an option to create pages and publish them as news, however, there is no mechanism to notify the users that something new was posted.

The SharePoint News connector allows you to automatically post news in a channel when it is published on SharePoint. This app is not pre-installed on Microsoft Teams and needs to be added from the store. To do so, follow these steps:

1. Open Microsoft Teams and click on **Apps**.

2. Search for `SharePoint News` and click on the app with this name when it appears.

3. Click on **Add to team**.

4. Select the team where you want to add the connector.

5. Click on **Set up connector** and then **Save**.

The connector will do the configuration automatically and will connect to the SharePoint site collection associated to the team. This connector will only work on standard channels – private channels and site collections do not include the News feature:

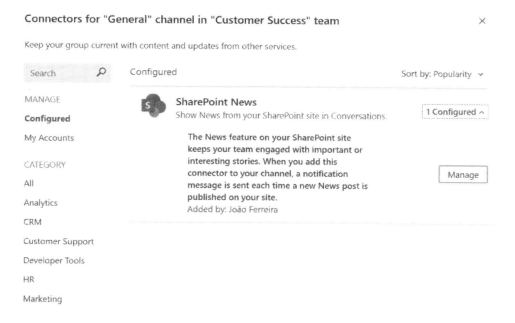

Figure 7.17: SharePoint News connector

The news is posted in the channel using a card format and when the user clicks on it, they are redirected to the news in the browser, as illustrated in the following screenshots:

Figure 7.18: SharePoint News posts in Microsoft Teams

SharePoint

The SharePoint app allows you to add pages and lists to a channel from the site collection of the team. It has a simple configuration interface where you are able to select the list or the page you want to display, as shown in the following screenshot:

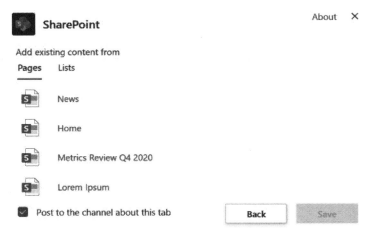

Figure 7.19: SharePoint list selection

A modern SharePoint page is designed to be displayed inside of Microsoft Teams. This means that the page will be displayed without the logo and navigation; it will only display the web parts (web parts on SharePoint are the equivalent to apps on Microsoft Teams) you have in the page.

Unlike the document library, this app does not allow you to select pages or lists from other site collections, but as a workaround, you can use the Website app, which allows you to embed any web page into a tab.

The main difference between both applications is that on the configuration window, Website requires you to add the link manually. Visually, they are very similar, and the only thing you will notice when using Website is an info message at the top the page, as highlighted in the following screenshot:

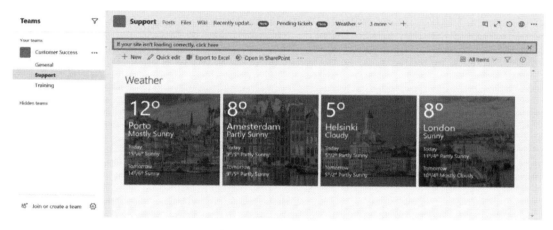

Figure 7.20: SharePoint list using the Website app

As a SharePoint user, you will be able to integrate both platforms using the out-of-the-box apps. As we will see in *Chapter 8, Build Your Own App for Microsoft Teams Using App Studio,* there is much more you can do with SharePoint and Microsoft Teams to build a reliable and centralized modern workplace.

In our next section, we will see how to build our own custom apps using Power Automate.

Extending Microsoft Teams using Power Automate

Microsoft Power Automate (formerly known as Microsoft Flow) is a tool that allows us to create automated workflows without writing code. It has more than 300 connectors divided between a free and a premium plan.

> **Note:**
> Most of the connectors from Microsoft 365 are included in the free plan and you can use it as part of your existing subscription without extra costs.

One of the free integrations available is Microsoft Teams, with which you can automate processes for you or your teams.

In this section of the book, you will learn, with the aid of examples, how easy it is to set up a workflow using Power Automate and also how they can be managed from the Microsoft Teams context.

> **Case study: Paul, the blog manager**
> Paul is the company WordPress blog manager and does all the posts and scheduling. To reach a broader internal audience, Paul wants each post to be promoted on the general channel that all the users have access to on Microsoft Teams.
>
> Since some of the posts are scheduled and Paul wants this task to be fully automated, he will use Power Automate to publish a message on the general channel with the title, date, and link for the new post.

The idea described in this scenario can be implemented by doing the following:

1. Open Microsoft Power Automate at `https://flow.microsoft.com/`.

2. On the vertical menu, click on **Create**.

3. On the **Create** menu, click on **Automated Flow**.

4. On the popup, provide a name for your flow.

5. Select the trigger. A trigger is an event that will start the flow execution. In this scenario, the blogging platform used is WordPress, so you need to select the trigger named **When a post is created**.

6. Click on **Create**:

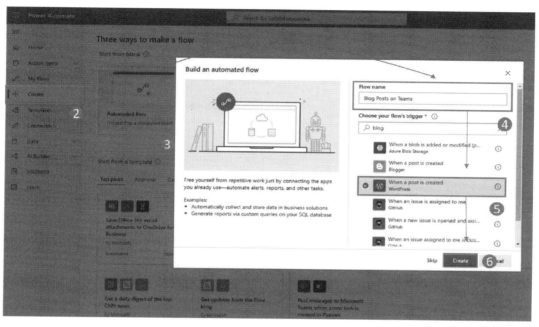

Figure 7.21: Building an automated flow

7. Authenticate on WordPress. This step is common to all the triggers from third-party connectors, as you need to grant permissions to Power Automate to let it access your data from a third-party platform.

8. At the flow stage, click on **New step**.

9. Search for Microsoft Teams.

10. Select the action named **Post your own adaptive card as the Flow bot to a channel**. Adaptive cards are built with JSON and are an easy way to post structured information on several Microsoft 365 platforms. Adaptive cards can be built visually using the designer tool (https://adaptivecards.io/designer/). Once you get the desired layout, you can copy the generated JSON and reuse it:

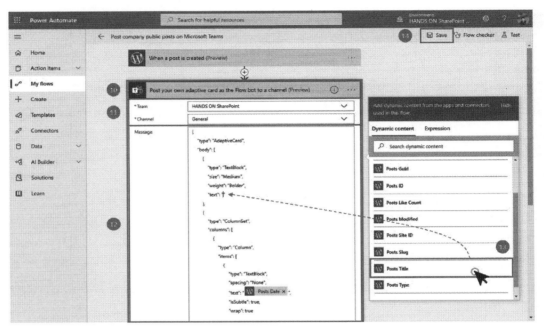

Figure 7.22: Posting an adaptive card

11. Select the team and the channel where you want to post the card.

12. In the **Message** text box, paste the JSON code.

13. Look for the placeholders where you want to add the text from the post and click on the corresponding post field. Fields are added to the JSON in the cursor location once you click on them.

14. Click on **Save**.

Every time this flow is executed, it will automatically post a message on Microsoft Teams using the card format you have built, as the following screenshot demonstrates. Posts are made by Power Automate and the card includes information about the author of the message:

Figure 7.23: Adaptive cards in Microsoft Teams

Microsoft Teams can be used for actions, as we have seen in this example, but it can also be used as a trigger. The following lists detail all the available integrations and even though some of them are still in preview, you should be able to use them without any issues.

Triggers:

- When a new channel message is added
- When I am mentioned in a channel message
- When a new member is added

Actions:

- Get messages: This action gets messages from a channel into a team.
- Post a choice of options as the Flow bot to a user: This action creates a card with a set of options that a user must choose before responding.
- Post a message: This message is posted into a team channel.
- Post a reply to a message.
- Create a channel.
- List Channels.
- List Teams: Lists the teams you are a member of.

- Post a message as the Flow bot to a channel.
- Post a message as the Flow bot to a user.
- Post an Adaptive Card to a Teams channel and wait for a response.
- Post an Adaptive Card as the Flow bot to a user.
- Post an Adaptive Card as to a Teams user and wait for a response.
- Post your own adaptive card as the Flow bot to a channel.
- Post your own adaptive card as the Flow bot to a user.

Power Automate can also be integrated with Microsoft Teams using an app available in the Microsoft Teams store.

> **Note**
> At the time of writing, the app is still available with the old name – Flow.

Flow is available as a personal app and as a tab, and allows you to build your automations directly from Microsoft Teams.

The personal app also gives you access to the approval list and to the bot that allows you to trigger your flows using natural language. The following screenshot displays the personal flow app, showing the user view of their own **Flows**:

Figure 7.24: Managing Flows from Microsoft Teams

The tab displays your team flows and also allows you and your team members to create new ones. When creating a new Teams flow using the **tab** app, it fills in the form automatically with the team and channel details. The following illustrates how the tab app looks in configuration mode:

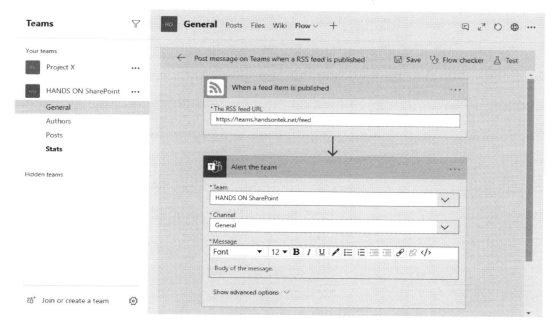

Figure 7.25: Creating a Flow from Microsoft Teams

Extending Microsoft Teams using PowerApps

Power Apps is a platform that empowers everyone to build business applications without writing code. With a simple and intuitive layout, it empowers every user to build more to achieve more. Microsoft Teams wants to embrace the power of apps created by users and allows you to use them on the platform. This way, we can say that every Power App is also a Teams app.

> **Note:**
> This section of the book does not cover the creation of an app; it only shows how you can integrate an existent app into Microsoft Teams.

Let's now take a look at a scenario to understand this better.

> **Case study: Adele, the event manager**
>
> Adele is responsible for all the events at the company and has a budget to manage during the year. To help her with all the events and with the visualization of how much is being spent on each one, Adele has created a PowerApp based on the data she already had.
>
> Now that the app is working, Adele wants to share it with her team members so everyone can be aware of how much was spent.

Power Apps is available on Microsoft Teams as a tab only. This means that you can only use it in a channel or in a chat context. Every time you add a Power App to Microsoft Teams, you should guarantee that all the users will have access to the original Power App.

To start adding a Power App to one of your teams, do the following:

1. Go to the app store, search for `PowerApps`, and click on it.

2. Select the **Channel** or the **Chat** that you want to add it to.

3. Establish the connection between Power Apps and Microsoft Teams – this is necessary to get access to your apps.

4. Select the app you want to add:

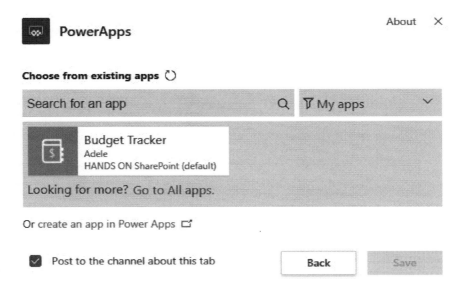

Figure 7.26: Adding an app to Microsoft Teams

5. Click on **Save**.

The app is added to a tab showing the original name you gave to it on Power Apps, and the layout will reflect exactly what you did on the original app. The following screenshot displays the Power Apps app behaving as a native Teams app:

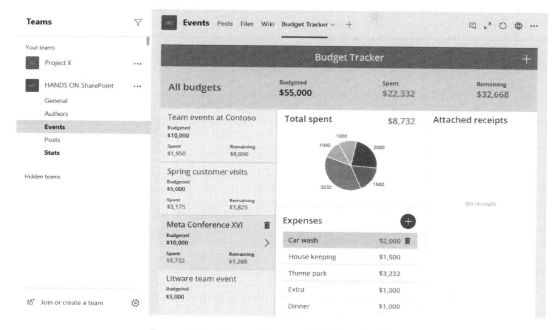

Figure 7.27: A Power Apps app in Microsoft Teams

If you don't want to add the app to a team but instead want to use it as a personal app, you will need to download the application package from the PowerApps application itself. To do this, do the following:

1. Open the PowerApps website at `https://make.powerapps.com/`.

2. From the vertical menu, click on **Apps**.

3. Select the app you want to install and click on the ... button to open the **More options** menu.

4.   Click on **Add to Teams**:

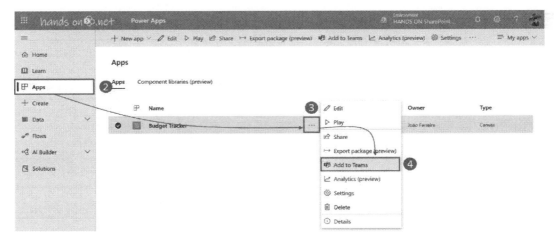

Figure 7.28: Adding an app to Microsoft Teams from Power Apps

5.   From the vertical menu, click on **Download app**:

Figure 7.29: Downloading a Power Apps app

6.   Save the ZIP file.

7.   Upload the application package to Microsoft Teams, as described in the *Installing custom apps* section.

Once uploaded and installed, you will be able to access to your Power Apps app from the vertical app menu, as shown in the following screenshot:

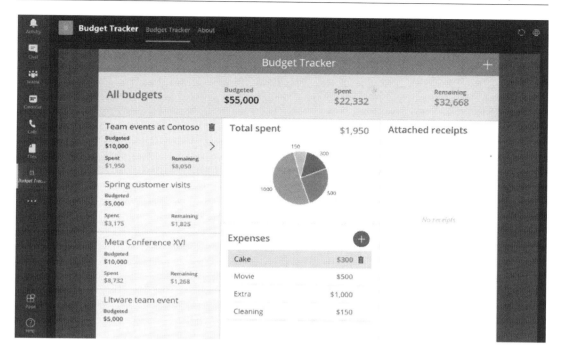

Figure 7.30: A Power Apps app in Microsoft Teams as a personal app

Summary

In this chapter, you have learned how to extend Microsoft Teams in a more advanced way using the tools and platforms that are included on the Microsoft 365 platform. We also demonstrated, through the use of scenarios, how you can integrate the collaboration and communication areas of a modern workplace by building custom apps without writing code.

In the next chapter, we will continue to explore the options available to extend Microsoft Teams, and you will learn how to create a personal app from scratch without writing code.

8

Build Your Own App for Microsoft Teams Using App Studio

So far, we have seen how Microsoft Teams can be extended using apps from the store and apps developed by third-party developers. In this chapter, we will continue to see how Microsoft Teams can be further extended and how you can build your own applications.

Anyone can be a citizen developer on the Microsoft Teams ecosystem, and with Microsoft Teams App Studio you will be able to build your own apps and integrate your own tools inside Teams.

In the following pages, you will find information about these main topics:

- Understanding Microsoft Teams App Studio
- Getting familiar with Microsoft Teams App Studio
- Building an app using App Studio
- Using App Studio to integrate SharePoint and Microsoft Teams

Understanding Microsoft Teams App Studio

There are thousands of applications outside of the Microsoft ecosystem that are used by organizations in their day-to-day tasks; however, most of them don't have an integration with Microsoft Teams, which forces you to use them in a standalone mode.

Microsoft is well aware of this and wants to empower you to build/bring your business applications and scenarios to the Microsoft Teams context. To help with this, Teams has built App Studio.

Microsoft Teams App Studio is an app built by Microsoft to develop apps easily and quickly. Using this app, you will be able to create your own personal apps and tabs and you will also get access to some of the documentation about the design language of Microsoft Teams apps.

This simple app can be used by any citizen developer to build their own app in a matter of a few clicks. Now that we have understood the basics of what App Studio is, we will learn about its different features and get familiar with how to use it.

Getting familiar with Microsoft Teams App Studio

In order to accomplish the steps described in this chapter, third-party apps must be enabled in the **Org-wide app settings** in the Microsoft Teams admin center, as shown here:

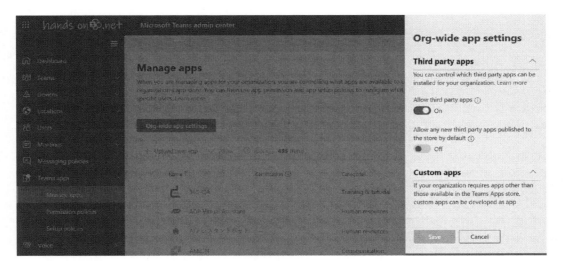

Figure 8.1: Enable third-party apps

> **Note**
>
> More details about managing apps can be found in *Chapter 7, Extend Microsoft Teams Using Custom Apps and Microsoft 365.*

Microsoft Teams App Studio is a personal app and needs to be installed to be used in the organization. To get access to the studio environment, follow these steps:

1. Open the **Microsoft Teams** store by clicking on the store icon in the app bar.

2. Search for App Studio and click on it.

3. Click on **Add**. After a few seconds, the app will be ready to use:

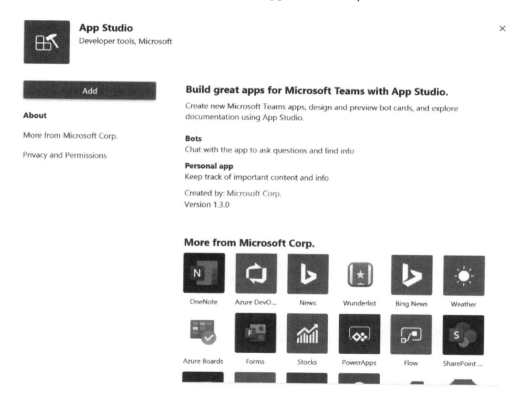

Figure 8.2: Adding App Studio

4. To open the app, click on **...** in the app bar and then in the more apps menu, click on **App Studio**.

Now that you have App Studio installed, you need to get familiar with it before we start using it. In the following sections, you will find a detailed explanation of all the features.

Chat

In the **chat** tab of App Studio, you will be able to interact with the bot to get information about how to develop apps and documentation. In the following screenshot, the bot was asked for information about the messaging extensions, and it returned links to relevant Microsoft articles:

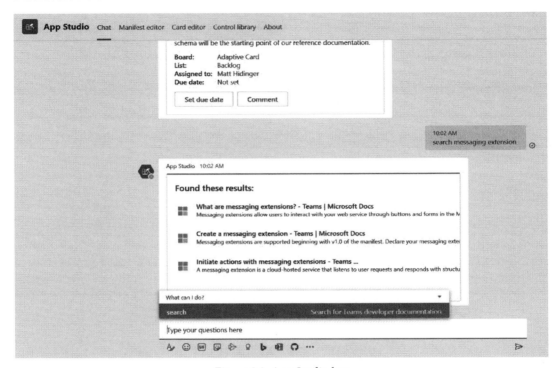

Figure 8.3: App Studio bot

In this chat section, you will also be able to test other features that can be built using the App Studio, like the cards and adaptive cards used in the Power Automate example in *Chapter 7, Extend Microsoft Teams Using Custom Apps and Microsoft 365*. This way, you will be able to get a preview of what it will look like when added to a chat window.

Manifest editor

The Manifest editor is the tab that allows you to build your own apps. It gives you access to the form with all the necessary options to generate a Microsoft Teams app. Behind the scenes, it generates a JSON file that can be then installed in your tenant directly or downloaded and uploaded into other tenants. The following screenshot shows what the **Manifest editor** tab looks like:

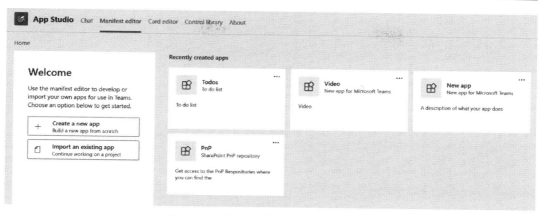

Figure 8.4: App Studio – Manifest editor

Card editor

The card editor allows you to generate cards and adaptive cards to include in your Microsoft Teams integration, as we saw in *Chapter 7, Extend Microsoft Teams Using Custom Apps and Microsoft 365* with Power Automate. If you are planning an automated way to post messages have a look at this section; it will allow you to build the card, preview what it looks like, and get the code in three different formats: JSON, C#, and Node.

While building the card, you can test how it will behave in a real chat window. When you click on the **Send me this card** button, the card is posted in the App Studio chat:

Figure 8.5: App Studio – Card editor

Control library

If you know how to write code and want to build the most amazing native Microsoft Teams app you definitely need to check out the control library. Here, you will find all the controls that you will need to integrate in your app to make it look like a native Microsoft Teams application. The following screenshot shows all the options available in the **Control library** tab:

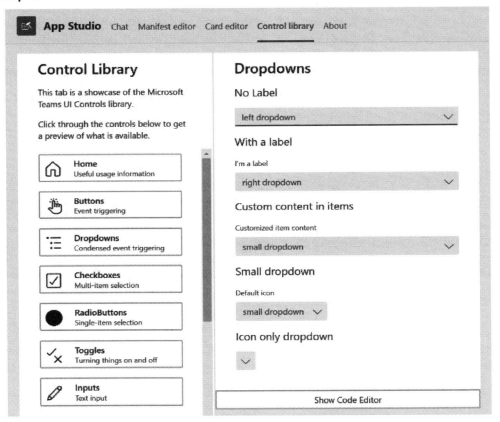

Figure 8.6: App Studio – Control Library

Now that we are familiar with all our features and how to use App Studio, in the next section we will see how to build an app with it.

Building an app using App Studio

Building your first app using App Studio is an easy task. All you have to do is get the links to the applications or to the sites that you want to embed into Microsoft Teams and follow the instructions described in this section.

> **Note**
>
> App Studio can be used to build all five types of apps (personal apps, bots, tabs, connectors, messaging)but the only ones that can be built without writing code and that are accessible to all citizen developers are personal apps, which are the focus of this section.

Let's now look at a scenario to understand how to use the App Studio better:

> **John the surfer**
>
> John loves to surf and recently opened his own surfing school. John and the other teachers need to regularly check the conditions of the sea before the classes.
>
> John's license allows him to teach on five different beaches, but visiting each one of them daily takes a lot of time. Luckily, those beaches are monitored 24/7 and live streamed on the internet, so John has decided to build his own app to get instant access to the videos while working and planning his day on Microsoft Teams.

If, like John, you also need a custom app on Microsoft Teams, follow these steps:

1. Open Microsoft Teams App Studio.

2. Click on the **Manifest editor** and then **Create a new app**.

3. Fill in the **App details** form. This is a long form, but there are a few fields that you can ignore if you are building the app for yourself. If you plan to publish it on the store, you should fill all the options according to the instructions to prevent the app being rejected:

    (a) **Short name**: The short name can have a maximum of 30 characters and is the name that is displayed in the app bar.

    (b) **Full name**: The full name allows you to exceed the 30 characters and is displayed when the app is visualized in the store. This field is mandatory and cannot be a copy of the short name if you want to submit the app to the store. However, if you want to use it on your own tenant you can use the same text as the short name and ignore the warnings.

    (c) **App ID** : This is the unique identifier for the app. This must be a GUID and can be generated when you click on the **Generate** button.

    (d) **Package Name**: The package name is a unique name that identifies your app, for example, com.domain.app

(e) **Version**: The current version of the app. Make sure you update the version every time you deploy the app in the app store. If you try to reinstall an app with the same version number, an error will occur.

(f) **Short Description**: The short description is displayed when the app is visualized in the store. It has a limit of 80 characters.

(g) **Full Description**: The full description is displayed in App Source (App Source is the general Microsoft marketplace for applications). This field is mandatory and cannot be a copy of the short description if you want to submit the app to the store. If you want to use it on your own tenant you can use the same text as the short description and ignore the warnings.

(h) **Developer Name**: The name of the person/company who developed the app.

(i) **Developer Website**: The public portal for the person/company who developed the app.

(j) **MPN ID**: This field is meant to be used just by Microsoft Partners. Microsoft uses the MPN ID to measure the usage of the apps built by each partner.

(k) **Privacy Statement**: This is a link to the public privacy policy. It must be a real privacy policy if you want to submit the app to the store. If you want to use it locally and don't have a privacy policy, you can, for instance, point it to your company website.

(l) **Terms of use**: A link to the terms of use. This must be a real document with terms if you want to submit the app to the store. If you want to use it locally and don't have one, you can, for instance, point it to your company website.

(m) **Full color logo** : This is the logo that will be visible on the store and on Microsoft Teams when the app is not pinned to the app bar. The size of the logo must be exactly 192x192 pixels.

(n) **Transparent outline**: This is the logo that is used when the app is pinned to the app bar. This logo must be an outline of the original logo in white and it must be exactly 32x32 pixels. If you want to submit your app to the store and your outline is not white and transparent, the app will fail the submission process. However, if you want to use it locally you will be able to use a color image.

(o) **Accent color**: This color is used as the background for the logo:

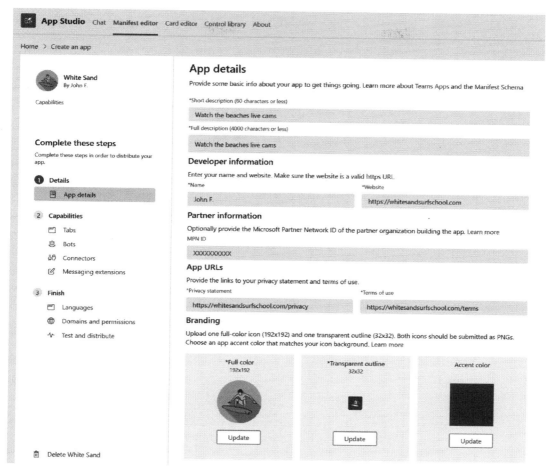

Figure 8.7: App details

4. In the second section, click on **Capabilities | Tabs**. In this section, you will be able to add tabs to the personal app, up to a maximum of sixteen.

5.   In the personal tab section, click on **Add**:

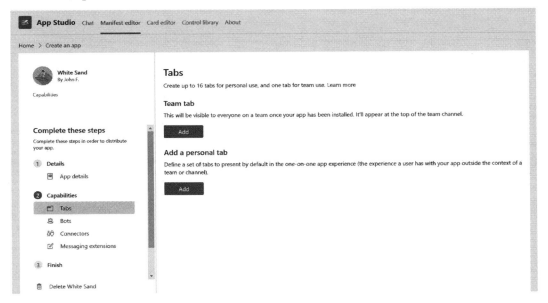

Figure 8.8: Tabs

6.   Fill the tab form. All the fields are mandatory:

(a) **Name**: The name displayed on the tab. This name cannot be modified by the users in the app, so make sure you pick something related to what will be displayed on the tab. The name for your tab should have a maximum of 18 characters. After this limit, the name will be displayed with ….

(b) **Entity ID**: The unique ID for the tab. Each tab inside the app needs to have its own ID.

(c) **Content URL**: The URL that will be rendered inside Microsoft Teams.

(d) **Website URL**: The URL where the users are redirected when they click on the option to open the tab in the browser:

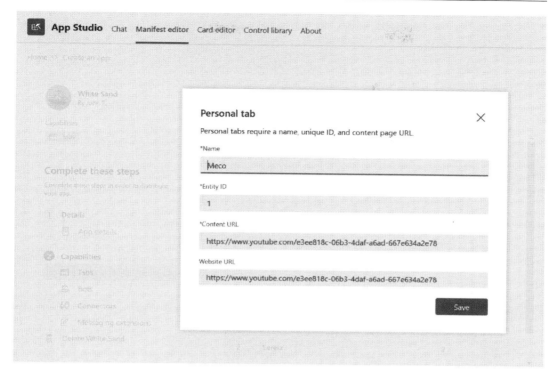

Figure 8.9: Creating a personal tab

Repeat steps 5 and 6 for all the tabs you want to add to your app.

7. Once you finish adding your tabs, move to the third and final section, Finish.

8. If your app will be supported in multiple languages, add the translation files in the **Languages** section. In personal apps, you will be able to submit a JSON file with the translation for the tab names.

In this section, you will find a template that can be downloaded and modified for each new language. In the following screenshot, you can see that a translation file for Portuguese has been added:

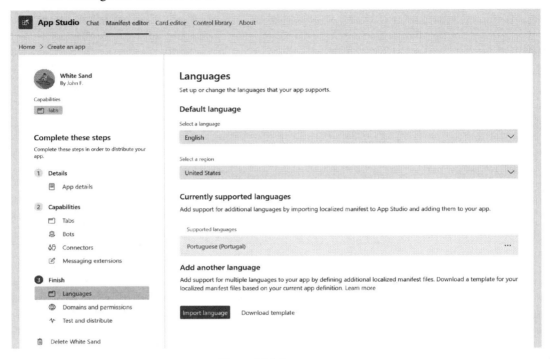

Figure 8.10: Languages

9. Click on **Domains and permissions** and make sure the domains used on your tab are listed in the domain list. By default, App Studio adds the domains from the tabs to this list, but if your app navigates to a different domain it should also be added in the **Valid domains** section.

Remember, the domain list is not updated when you remove tabs. Before installing the app, make sure the domains on the list are all being used in tabs. Unused domains can be deleted manually:

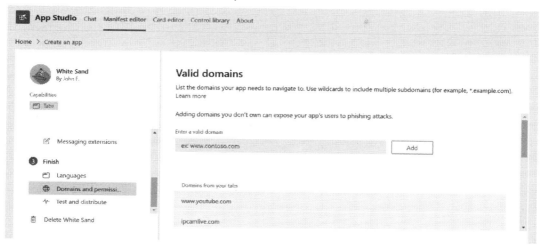

Figure 8.11: Domains

10. If you are ready to test or to use your app, click on **Test and distribute**. In this section, you will get the option to install the app directly in your tenant, download the ZIP file to install it in any other tenant, or start the process of submitting it to the store.

> **Note**
>
> To install the app, custom apps must be enabled for the user building the app. If you need help on how to enable custom apps, go to *Chapter 7, Extend Microsoft Teams Using Custom Apps and Microsoft 365.*

In this section, you will also find any errors or warning that may exist in your app, as the following screenshot shows. If you want to submit the app to the store, make sure that you don't have any warnings on this page; otherwise, the app will fail the submission process:

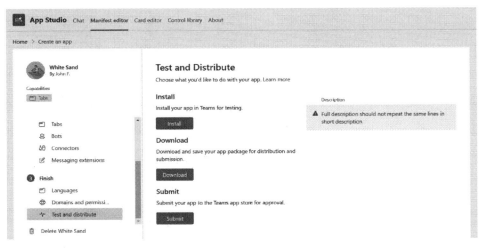

Figure 8.12: Test and distribute

These were the steps that John followed to build the app for his surf school. Since he only wanted to use it on this tenant he installed the app directly from App Studio. The end result is illustrated in the following screenshot. John made an app with five tabs that show all the spots where he can give surfing classes:

Figure 8.13: White Sand custom personal app

However, not all web applications will support the integration inside of Microsoft Teams. There are web applications that prevent being embedded inside other domains. Unfortunately, App Studio is not able to tell you whether the link you are adding is supported or not, but an unsupported page will look like this:

Figure 8.14: Error embedding a site in Microsoft Teams custom app

Using App Studio to integrate SharePoint and Microsoft Teams

As we have seen, building personal apps using Microsoft Teams is a really simple process, but if you want to build your own app using SharePoint there are a few things that you will have to take care of.

If you create the app using SharePoint pages just using the URL you copied from the browser, you will end up with an app that will only work on the web version of Microsoft Teams. On the desktop and mobile clients, the user will end up on a blank page without the option to sign in to SharePoint.

To overcome this limitation, it is necessary to use a hidden authentication page hosted in SharePoint:

1. Open App Studio and create or edit an existing app.

2. When creating the tabs, modify the **Content URL** to the following format: `https://handsonsp.sharepoint.com/_layouts/15/teamslogon.aspx?spfx=true&dest=/sites/projects/SitePages/It's-all-about-communication.aspx`.

3. The link to the actual page is added as a relative URL after the `dest` parameter in the URL. Leave the **Website URL** as the default SharePoint link:

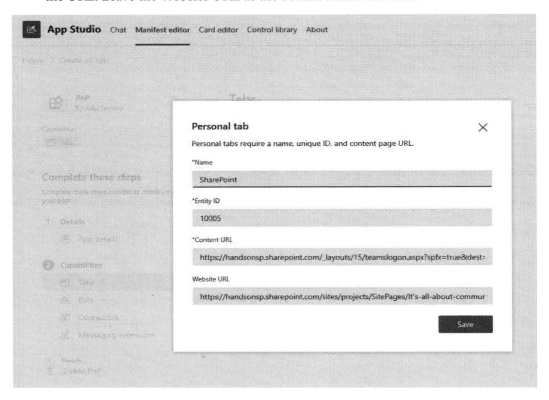

Figure 8.15: SharePoint personal tab with the login details

4. For the domains and permissions, add the following domains manually by clicking on the **Add** button:

    ```
    *.login.microsoftonline.com
    *.sharepoint.com
    *.sharepoint-df.com
    spoppe-a.akamaihd.net
    spoprod-a.akamaihd.net
    resourceseng.blob.core.windows.net
    msft.spoppe.com
    ```

> **Note: Wildcard domains**
>
> Wildcard domains, such as the ones in this list, will cause a warning and are not allowed if you want to submit your app to the store. All the domains in this list are from Microsoft and are safe domains. However, if while building your app you need to use wildcard domains, make sure they are safe, otherwise you may compromise the security of your application.

The following screenshot shows how we can add Microsoft domains:

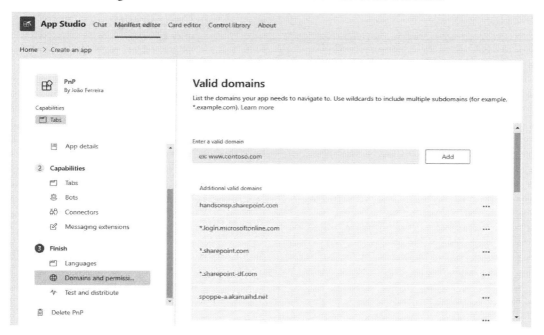

Figure 8.16: Microsoft domains

5. In the domains and permissions, scroll down and add the following value to the **AAD AppID** field:

    `00000003-0000-0ff1-ce00-000000000000`

    This app already exists on your Azure tenant and is used also by the SPFx web parts on Microsoft Teams.

    > **Note**
    >
    > As mentioned in the previous chapter, web parts on SharePoint are the equivalent to apps on Microsoft Teams.

6. In the domain permission, add the URL to your SharePoint portal to the **Single-Sign-On** field:

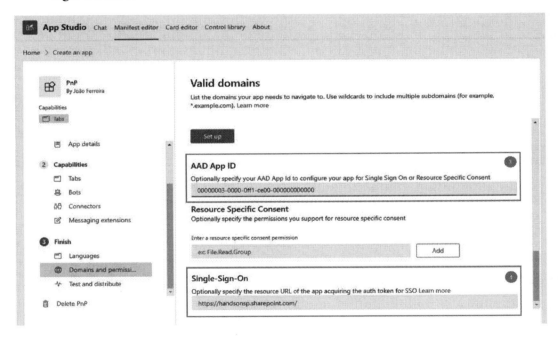

Figure 8.17: AAD App ID

7. Save the app and install it.

The use of the resources of the SharePoint web parts explained in this section will force your Teams app to do silent authentication. This way, the content from SharePoint will be displayed as a native Microsoft Teams app.

Summary

In this chapter, you have learned how to build your own personal apps to extend Microsoft Teams using the App Studio in Microsoft Teams itself. Through these step-by-step examples, are be able to incorporate third-party web applications into Microsoft Teams, and you are also now able to create your own personal app using SharePoint.

In the next chapter, we will continue to explore the options to extend Microsoft Teams and you will learn how to create your own bot.

9
Building Your Own Bot for Microsoft Teams

If you were to say in your organization that you were going to build a bot to automate any tasks, I'm sure you would gain the attention of everyone in the room. Bots are powerful automated agents that can help you to do your daily tasks in an efficient way using natural language.

Even though it sounds futuristic and complex, building a bot is quite easy and does not require a single line of code. It is also quite easily accessible to everyone. By the end of this chapter, you will hopefully be the Microsoft Teams superhero of your organization.

The topics you will learn about in this chapter are as follows:

- Creating and packaging a bot using QnA Maker
- Creating and packaging a bot using Power Virtual Agents
- Using a bot in Microsoft Teams

Creating a bot using QnA Maker

Creating a bot for Microsoft Teams is only a few clicks away from any citizen developer using Microsoft QnA Maker, Microsoft Azure, and Microsoft Teams App Studio.

Microsoft QnA Maker is a service that allows you to build and publish bots without writing code. Using an intelligent extraction system, it is able to get the information to be used by the bot from an Excel spreadsheet, a Word document, or even a website.

Before we begin creating our bot, you will need to have access to your organization's Microsoft Azure and you must be able to deploy custom apps on Microsoft Teams.

> **Peter – HR manager**
>
> Peter manages HR in his organization and spends most of his day replying to questions from other employees. To save him time, Peter has compiled questions and replies in an Excel file, from which he copies them into Microsoft Teams.
>
> To get more time to do his daily tasks, Peter wants to build a Microsoft Teams bot to reply to questions automatically, and to achieve this, he will use Microsoft QnA Maker.

If, like Peter, you see yourself building a bot, follow these steps and you will be able to do it in under 60 minutes. So let's begin:

1. Start by opening QnA Maker – `https://www.qnamaker.ai/`.

2. Click on **Sign in** and authenticate using your corporate account:

Figure 9.1: QnA Maker website

3. Once authenticated, in the black bar at the top, click on **Create a knowledge base**. This action will redirect you to a five-step process in which you will create the intelligence for your bot.

4. In **STEP 1 Create a QnA service in Microsoft Azure**, click on the **Create a QnA service** button. This action will open Microsoft Azure and, if you're not yet authenticated, you must sign in with your corporate account:

Figure 9.2: Create a QnA service

5. In Azure, you will be presented with a form similar to the one in the following screenshot, which you must fill in to create your QnA service:

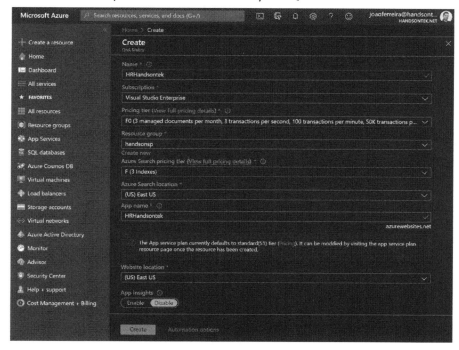

Figure 9.3: QnA creation form

(a) **Name**: The name that will identify your QnA service on Azure.

(b) **Subscription**: If you have access to more than one Azure subscription, select the one you want to use here.

(c) **Pricing tier**: Select the pricing tier. There are several options available. Choose one according to the load you estimate for your bot. The F tier is free and gives you 3 transactions per second and a maximum of 50,000 transactions per month. You can start with the free instance and adjust it later if needed.

(d) **Resource group**: The resource group where you want to create your service. Resource groups on Azure are typically used to group resources related to the same application or to separate resources from production and development environments.

(e) **Azure Search pricing tier**: Azure Search is a cognitive service that will be used by the bot. This is the service that handles the natural language and retrieves the results even if the question is not an exact match to what was provided to the QnA service. The F tier is free. It gives you 50 MB of storage. If needed, you can adjust it later to a paid tier with more storage space.

(f) **Azure Search location**: The data center where your service will be running. It's recommended to select the one closer to the physical location of your organization.

(g) **App Name**: The name of your app service. By default, it will have the same name as the QnA service, but you can change it if needed.

(h) **Website location**: The data center where your website will be located. It's recommended to select the one closest to the physical location of your organization.

(i) **App insights**: App insights is a tool that helps you to understand how your app is being used. It will monitor the usage of the application so you will know what your users are doing with your bot.

6. Click on **Create**. The service will take a few minutes to get created. Once it's available, you will receive a notification on Azure.

Go back to the QnA Maker portal, scroll down to **STEP 2 Connect your QnA service to your KB**, and click the **Refresh** button. This will establish a connection with Azure and will get the information about the service you have just created. Select the service as shown in the following screenshot:

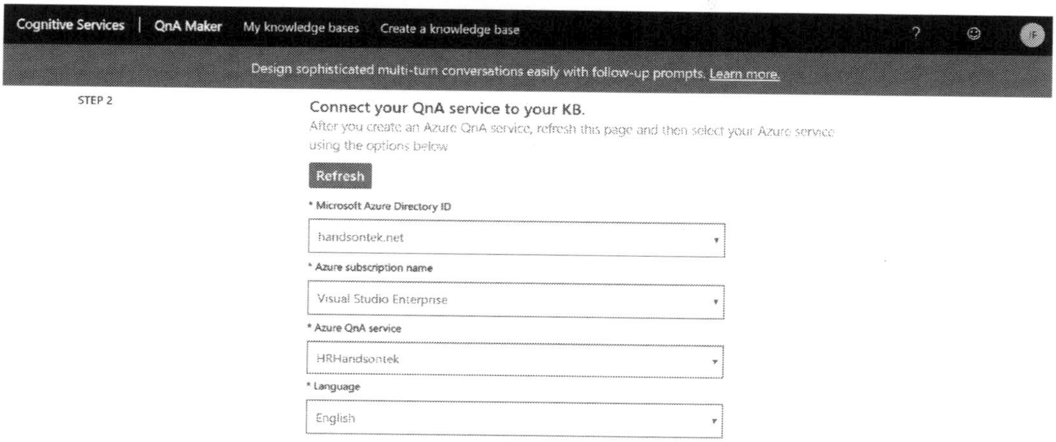

Figure 9.4: QnA connection

7. In **STEP 3 Name your KB**, provide a name for your knowledge base. This can be changed at any time if needed:

Figure 9.5: Knowledge base name

8. In **STEP 4 Populate your KB**, provide the data that your bot will use to answer the questions. This supports existing websites that will be parsed by the system to get questions, documents, and Excel spreadsheets.

9. Click on **Add file** and upload your Excel file. The following screenshot has an example of how simple your spreadsheet can be, with just two columns. In column A, we have the questions and in column B, we have the answers:

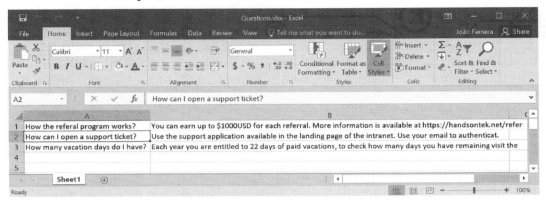

Figure 9.6: Excel questions and answers

10. Choose the **Chit-chat** option. By default, this option is off, but you can enable it to allow the bot to reply to questions that you have not planned to answer. There are five different types that you can choose from. Make sure you pick one that matches the culture of your organization:

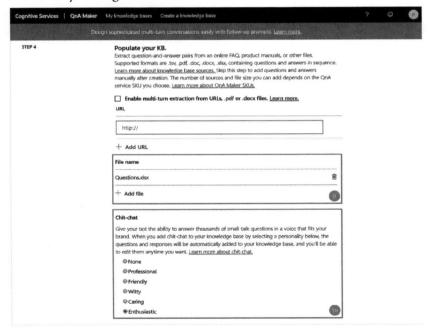

Figure 9.7: Knowledge base settings

11. In **STEP 5 Create your KB**, click on **Create your KB:**

Figure 9.8: Create knowledge base

12. After a few seconds, you will be redirected to the knowledge base **EDIT** panel and you will be able to review and add alternative phrases to your questions and answers.

13. Click on **Save and train**, to save any modifications you may have made to the system:

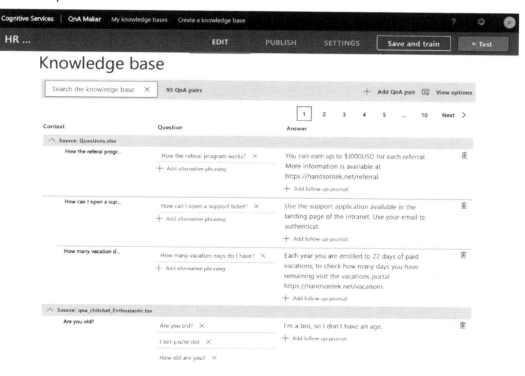

Figure 9.9: Knowledge base review

14. In the black bar at the top, click on **PUBLISH** and then click on the **Publish** button:

Figure 9.10: Publish knowledge base

15. After a few seconds, you will be redirected to a success page. On this page, click on the **Create Bot** button. This will redirect you to Azure again, where you will need to create the bot itself:

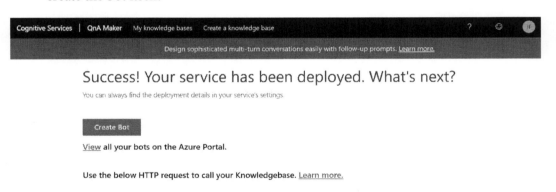

Figure 9.11: Deployment success

16. The form on Azure is automatically filled; you just need to validate the data and make the necessary adjustments. Since this is a no-code solution, you can ignore the option selected for **SDK language**:

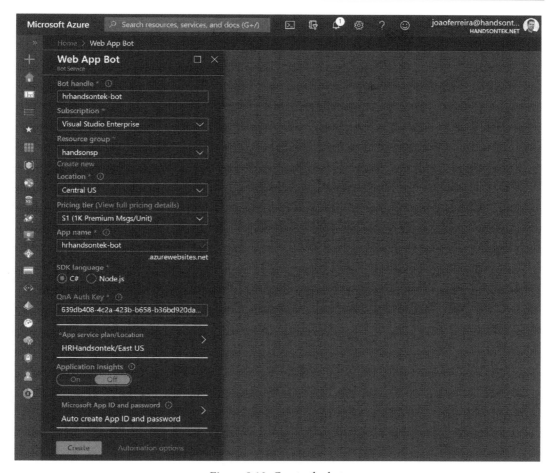

Figure 9.12: Create the bot

17. Click on **Create**. This process will take a few minutes. Once the deployment finishes, you will get a notification on Azure.

18. On the Azure notification, click on the **Go to resource** button. This will open the setup page of the bot framework:

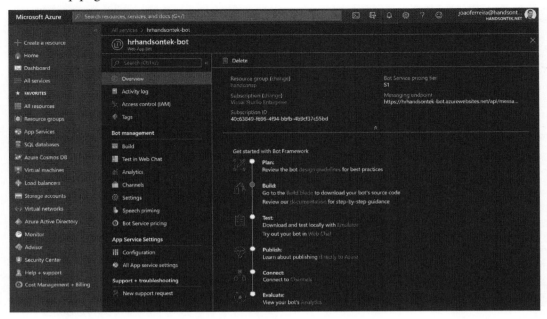

Figure 9.13: Bot framework setup

19. On the vertical menu, click on **Test in Web Chat** and check whether your bot works as you expect:

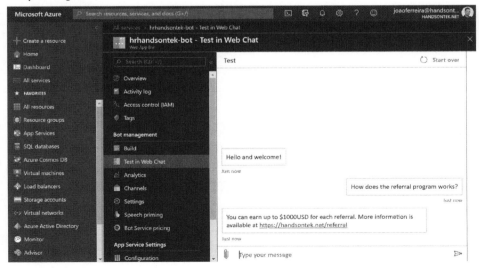

Figure 9.14: Test in Web Chat

20. On the vertical menu, click on **Channels** and then click on the Microsoft Teams logo:

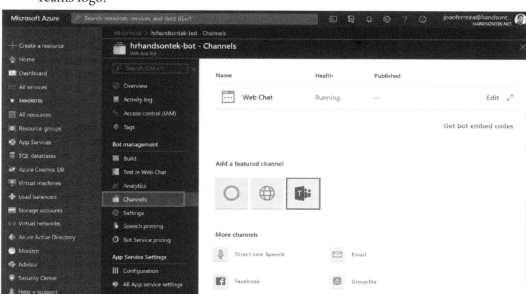

Figure 9.15: Add a Microsoft Teams channel

21. Click on **Save** to create a new channel for Microsoft Teams. This action will allow you to test your bot on Microsoft Teams.

Creating a QnA bot is accessible to all users if they have access to their organization's Microsoft Azure subscription. Also, it can be used to automate processes that are currently being done manually, wasting the productive time of all collaborators.

Packaging the bot using QnA Maker

To make your bot available to all users in the organization, you have to package it as an app. In this section, you will learn what steps are needed to package your first bot for Microsoft Teams.

> **Note**
> If you are not yet familiar with Microsoft Teams App Studio, it is recommended to have a look at *Chapter 8, Build Your Own App for Microsoft Teams Using App Studio*.

Let's get right to it:

1. Open App Studio on Microsoft Teams.

2. Click on the **Manifest editor** tab.

3. Click on the **Create a new app** button:

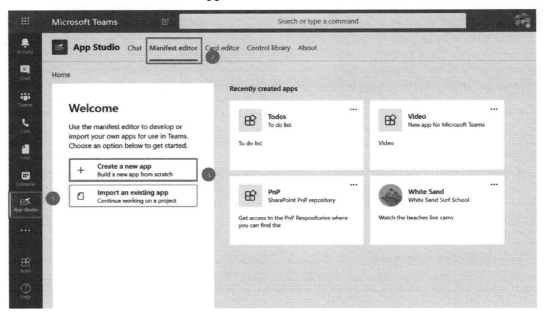

Figure 9.16: Create a new app

4. Fill in the **App details** form. A detailed description of this form can be found in *Chapter 8, Build Your Own App for Microsoft Teams Using App Studio.*

5. On the **Capabilities** group click on **Bots**.

6. To start the connection between your bot and your Microsoft Teams app, click on **Set up:**

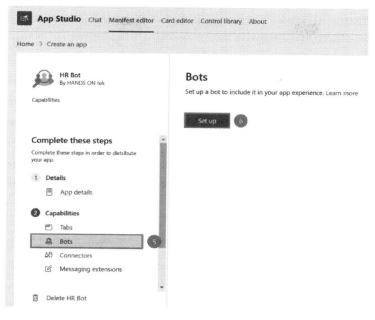

Figure 9.17: Setup bot

7.   On the **Set up a bot** popup, click on the **Existing bot** tab:

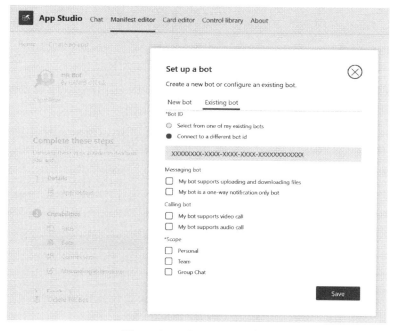

Figure 9.18: Connect to a bot

8. Select **Connect to a different bot id** and open Azure to get the ID of your bot.

9. On Azure, click on **All services**.

10. In the Overview menu, click on **AI + machine learning**.

11. Click on the name of your newly created bot:

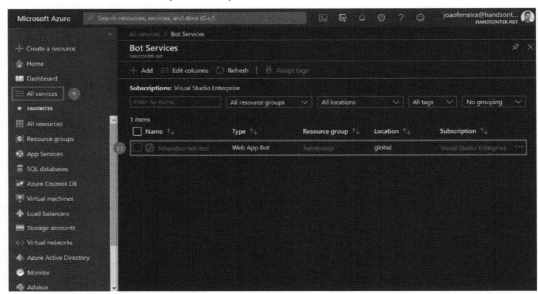

Figure 9.19: Web App Bot

12. On the **App Service Settings** group, click on **Configuration**.

13. On the **Application settings** tab, look for the value **MicrosoftAppId**.

14. Click on it and copy its value:

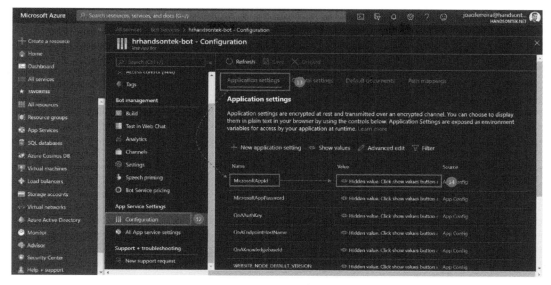

Figure 9.20: Copy bot ID

15. Paste the ID from Azure in the **Bot ID** field in Microsoft Teams App Studio.

16. On the **scope** option, select where you want to make it available. You can choose **Personal**, **Team**, or **Group** chat. Choose according to the features and the intent of your bot. The more options you select, the more possibilities you will give to your users to interact with it.

17. Click on **Save**.

18. On the **Finish** step, click on **Test and distribute**.

19. Click on **Download** to get the application package:

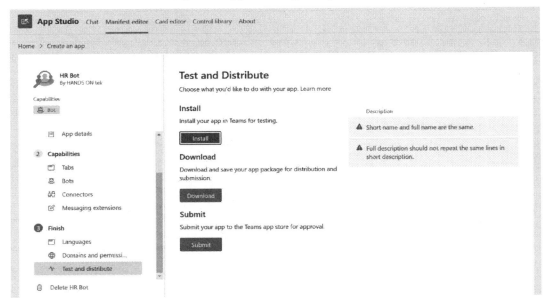

Figure 9.21: Download the bot app

20. Open Microsoft Teams Apps Store.

21. Click on **Upload a custom app**, and select the upload for the organization to make it available to all users.

22. Once installed, click on the app and then click **Add**. To learn more about how to install custom apps on Microsoft Teams, read *Chapter 6, Extending Microsoft Teams Using Apps*.

After completing these steps, your bot has been built with QnA Maker on Azure, and that was done without writing a single line of code. Similar to how we created a bot using QnA Maker, in the next section, we will see how to do so using another tool.

Creating a bot using Power Virtual Agents

Microsoft has different tools that allow you to rapidly create bots without writing code. We looked at QnA Maker in the previous section. Now we will have a look at Power Virtual Agents.

> **Note: Power Virtual Agents licensing**
>
> Power Virtual Agents is not included in Microsoft 365 plans – it requires a separate license for it to work. More information about prices can be found on the Power Virtual Agents website at `https://powervirtualagents.microsoft.com/`.

To get started with Power Virtual Agents, do the following:

1. Open the sign-in page: `https://powervirtualagents.microsoft.com`.

2. **Sign in** if you already have a license or start a trial by clicking on **Sign up free** or **Start free**:

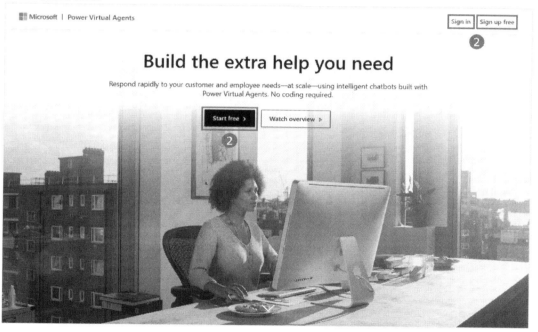

Figure 9.22: Sign in to Power Virtual Agents

3. On the **Create a new bot** popup, give your bot a name:

Figure 9.23: Create a new bot

4. Click on **Create** and wait a few seconds for the process to finish. Once it's created, you will enter Power Virtual Agents:

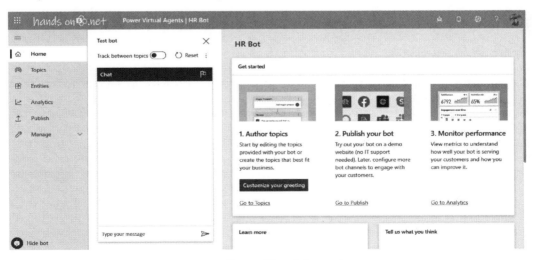

Figure 9.24: Power Virtual Agents layout

5. On the vertical menu, click on **Topics**. You will notice that the topics are already pre-populated with lessons that will help you to understand how Power Virtual Agents work with conditions and variables:

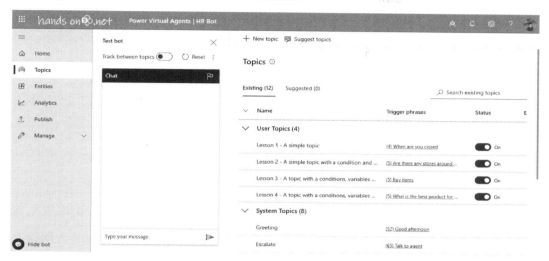

Figure 9.25: Topics

6. To add your own topic, click on **New topic**.

7. Provide a name and a description for your topic.

8. Enter a trigger phrase and click on **Add**. Try to start with 5-10 diverse phrases.

9. Click on **Go to authoring canvas** to start building your topic:

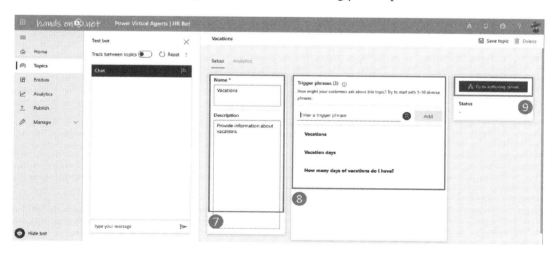

Figure 9.26: Create a new topic

10. Click on the + icon to add a node. Nodes can be messages, questions, or conditions:

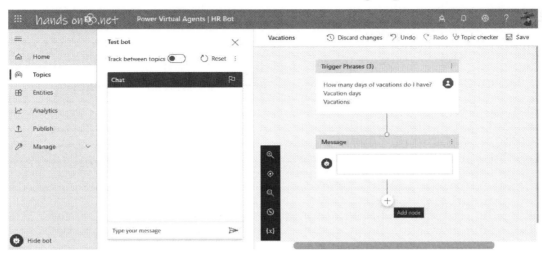

Figure 9.27: Authoring canvas

11. Build your topic as illustrated in the following screenshot and save it.

12. Test it in the test bot. The reply path will be highlighted in the build area:

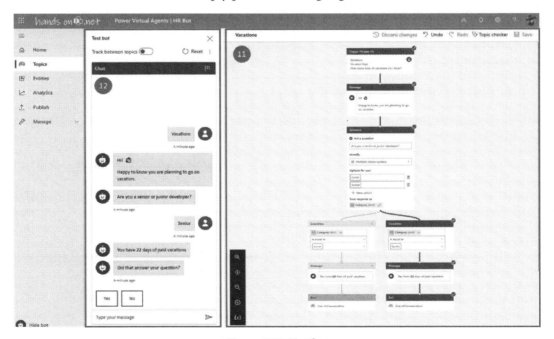

Figure 9.28: Test bot

Create as many topics as you need for your bot until it is ready to be added to Microsoft Teams.

Packaging the bot using Power Virtual Agents

The process to get your new bot packaged and installed on Teams is similar to the one we have seen already in the previous section, *Packaging the Bot using QnA Maker*. The main difference is in the steps required to get the bot's ID.

To get the bot's ID to package it into a Microsoft Teams app, do the following:

1. In the vertical menu, click on **Publish**.

2. In the **Publish** window, click on the **Publish** button. The publication will take 15 minutes:

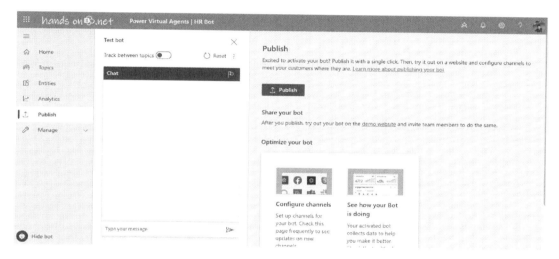

Figure 9.29: Publish

3. Scroll down and click on the **Go to channels** link.

4. Click on **Microsoft Teams**:

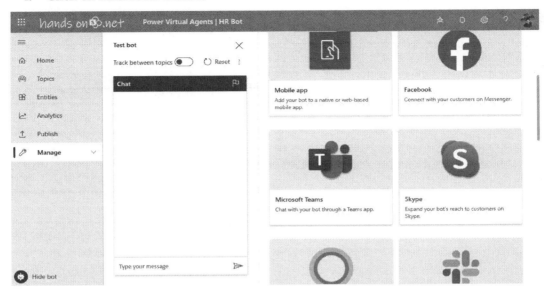

Figure 9.30: Channels

5. Click on **Add** to generate a new **App ID**.

6. Click on **Copy** to copy the app ID to the clipboard:

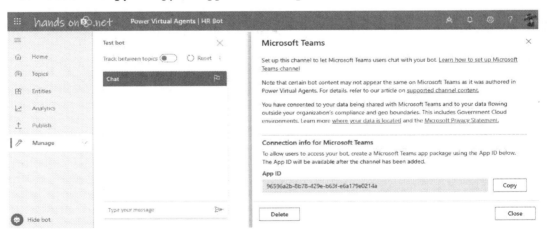

Figure 9.31: App ID

7. Follow the steps described in the *Packaging the bot created using QnA Maker* section (steps 1 to 7 and steps 19 to 22) to get the bot installed on Microsoft Teams.

Once packaged and installed, you will be able to interact with your virtual agent, as illustrated in the following screenshot:

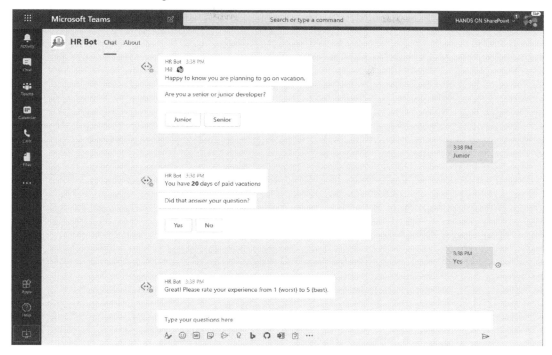

Figure 9.32: Power Virtual Agents bot running on Microsoft Teams

With Power Virtual Agents, you will be able to create complex scenarios for your bot without writing code. The graphical user interface allows you to easily see how things are working and how you can improve the replies of the bot.

Now that our bot is created and packaged, we are now ready to use it.

Using the bot on Microsoft Teams

Now that you have the bot installed on your tenant, you need to know how other members of the organization can interact with it.

Let's now see how to use the bot as a personal app:

1. You will need to click on **...** to expand the **More apps** section and get access to it:

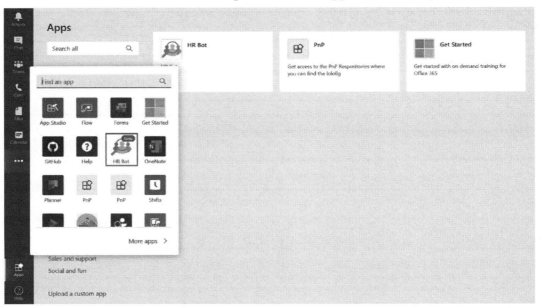

Figure 9.33: Installed bot on Microsoft Teams

Once you open the bot, you will be able to ask it private questions in a 1:1 chat without even mentioning the bot. Just type your question and wait for it to reply.

As you can see in the following screenshot, we have enabled the **Chit-chat** option so the bot is able to reply to questions other than the ones that were uploaded from the spreadsheet. This will make the user more comfortable when interacting with the bot:

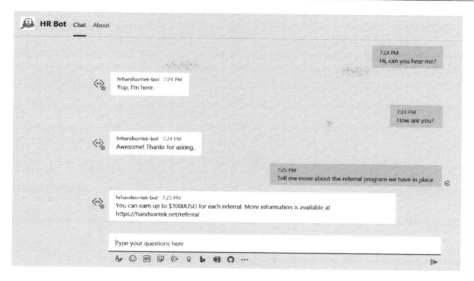

Figure 9.34: Bot interaction

The bot can also be used in the context of chats in channels and group chats. To use it, all you need to do is to mention it. Mentions on Microsoft Teams start with the @ sign followed by the name of the bot or the person.

In the following screenshot, you can see the bot being mentioned in a channel. The use of the bot in a channel allows you to keep a conversation about the same topic in one thread, as also illustrated in the screenshot:

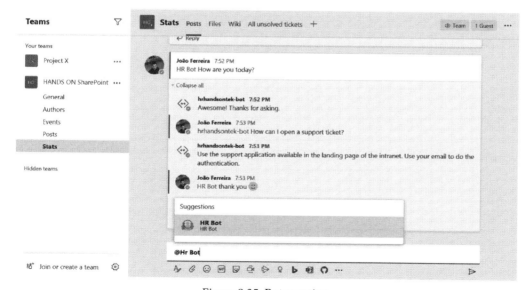

Figure 9.35: Bot mention

Summary

In this chapter, you have learned how to build your own bot with artificial intelligence and without writing a single line of code. You have also learned how to package the bot into a Microsoft Teams app, how to make it available in the tenant, and about the ways you can use it to interact with bots.

The last chapter of this book is for users that have an administrator role in their organization. It will cover Microsoft Teams PowerShell and will explain how you can automate tasks such as team creation in your organization using scripts.

10
Microsoft Teams PowerShell – a Tool for Automation

In this chapter, we will cover the PowerShell modules available to manage Microsoft Teams. This is the most advanced chapter of the book and will teach you how you can optimize administrative tasks while managing Teams.

The PowerShell modules can be very handy and save you a lot of time while managing teams, channels, users' apps, or even policies. In this chapter, you will cover the following topics:

- What is PowerShell and how can you use it?
- Installing Microsoft Teams PowerShell
- What are the available cmdlets in the Microsoft Teams module?
- Installing the Skype for Business PowerShell module
- What are the available cmdlets in the Skype for Business module?
- Learning how to use PowerShell from examples

What is PowerShell and how can you use it?

PowerShell is a command-line shell that gives you access to a framework to automate and configure processes on Windows.

First released in 2006, it is mainly used on Windows due to the technical architecture that was used in the earlier versions of PowerShell. It recently became available for other platforms, such as Linux and macOS, but most of the modules available do not support these operating systems.

Instructions on PowerShell are done through the use of cmdlets, where each cmdlet is responsible for the execution of a specific operation. Cmdlets can be combined into PowerShell scripts to automate scenarios, as we will see in this chapter.

A PowerShell script works like a programming language and you can create variables, conditions, or loops depending on the scenarios you want to automate. Scripts have the ps1 file extension and can be written with any text editor.

> **Note**
>
> This chapter assumes that the reader has a basic knowledge of development concepts and command line usage. If you are not familiar with programming concepts, you will find a nice book that explain all the basic concepts here: https://www.packtpub.com/application-development/introduction-programming

How to use PowerShell

In Microsoft Windows, if you open the start menu and type PowerShell, you will see that the system has multiple applications to work with PowerShell installed by default, as illustrated in the following diagram:

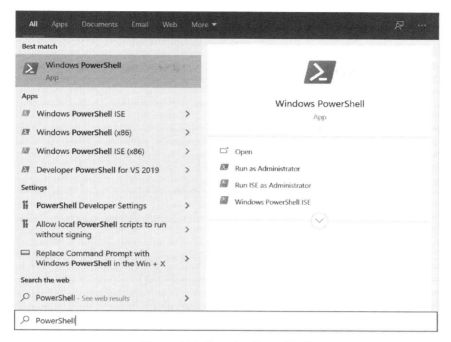

Figure 10.1: Opening PowerShell

Windows PowerShell is the console that allows you to execute single cmdlets, and the **Windows PowerShell ISE** is the editor that allows you to write automation scripts and test them.

To execute a PowerShell cmdlet, open the **Windows PowerShell** command line and type an instruction. Here's an example:

```
Get-Host | Select-Object Version
```

The following screenshot demonstrates how the instruction is run:

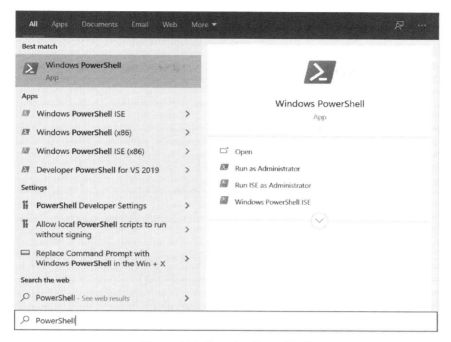

Figure 10.2: Executing PowerShell cmdlets

The execution of this cmdlet will print in the console the current version of PowerShell that is running on the operating system.

To build a script that executes several cmdlets, open the **Windows PowerShell ISE** and type your commands. Note that you can combine them with programming logic to format the outputs. The following script gets the version of PowerShell, and the version of Windows, and writes both on the screen:

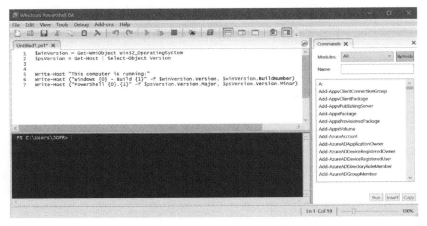

Figure 10.3: Windows PowerShell ISE

While writing your script, you can use the editor to test it. If you click on the play button, this will execute the code and will give you the result or the execution error in the console.

To execute a script that you have built and saved previously, you must open the Windows PowerShell command line. Once open, you need to navigate to the folder where the script is located and execute it using the following syntax:

```
./scriptName.ps1
```

The following screenshot displays the script execution and the results printed in the console:

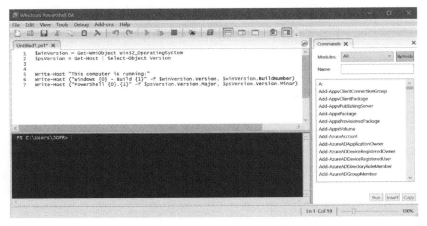

Figure 10.4: Script execution

In summary, we can say that PowerShell is a tool that allows the automation of repetitive tasks and has support for pretty much everything Microsoft-related. Now that you have been introduced to PowerShell, it's time to install the Microsoft Teams module.

Installing Microsoft Teams PowerShell

The PowerShell module for Microsoft Teams is not installed by default on Windows, so it needs to be added to the operating system.

Most of the official modules available can be found in the PowerShell gallery, a site where you can find a description for the module, installation instructions, and also the change log of each version. The PowerShell gallery is available at `https://www.powershellgallery.com/`.

To get the Microsoft Teams module installed in your system, perform the following steps:

1. On your computer, open the PowerShell command line with administrator permissions. To do so, search for Windows PowerShell on Windows and then select the option to **Run as Administrator**, as highlighted in the following screenshot:

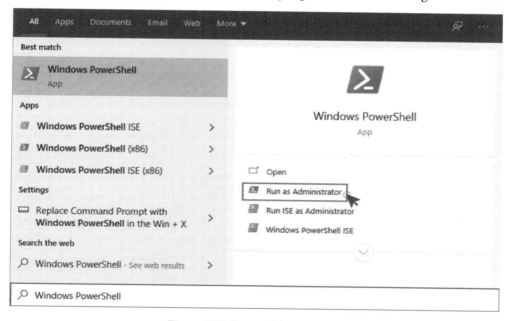

Figure 10.5: Run as Administrator

2. On the command line, execute the following command:

```
Install-Module -Name MicrosoftTeams
```

3. Type Y followed by *Enter* to trust and enter the repository:

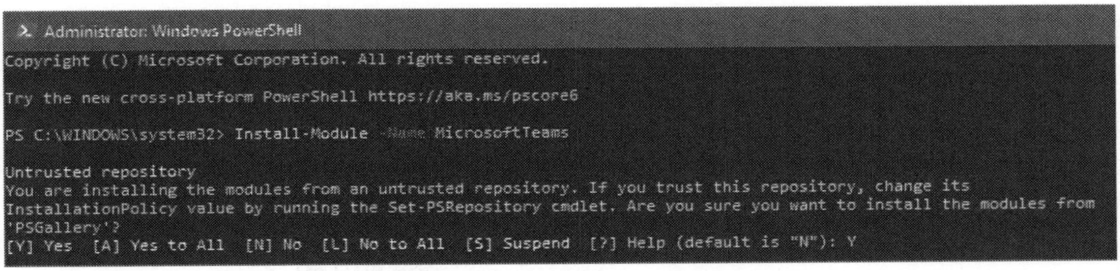

Figure 10.6: Installing the Microsoft Teams PowerShell module

4. Keep the console open while the download and installation are in progress.

Now that you have the Microsoft Teams module installed in your system, you are ready to start using it, but before doing so, you must know what cmdlets are available.

What are the available cmdlets in the Microsoft Teams module?

The cmdlets explained in this section are based on Microsoft Teams module 1.0.3 and they are divided into six different groups:

- Connection cmdlets
- Get cmdlets
- Set cmdlets
- New cmdlets
- Add cmdlets
- Remove cmdlets

In the following sections, you will find the name of the cmdlet, a description of it, and all the parameters you can use. The parameters are not explained in detail as the name is self-explanatory. Each parameter is followed by the data type it receives.

> **Data types**
>
> To better understand the cmdlets described in this section, check the data types used by PowerShell:
>
> `String`: A string is used to represent text. In PowerShell, a string can be represented in the following format: `This is a string.`
>
> `Boolean`: A Boolean is used to represent true or false. In PowerShell, Boolean values are represented in the following format: `$true` or `$false`.

While working with PowerShell, you can use the cmdlet `Show-Command` that will allow you to introduce the parameters through a graphical user interface. `Show-Command` is a very handy tool when you are still learning a PowerShell module, or you simply don't know what parameters a cmdlet receives. `Show-Command` is used in the following format:

```
Show-Command -name "Get-Team"
```

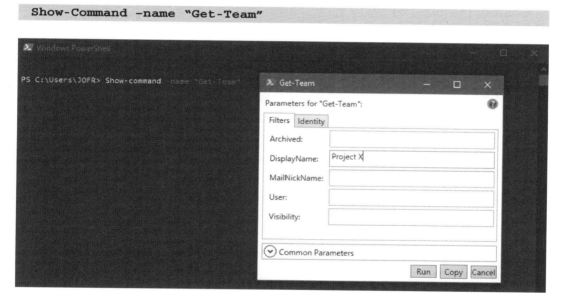

Figure 10.7: Show-command cmdlet

Connection cmdlets

The descriptions and parameters of the connection cmdlets are as follows:

- **Connect-MicrosoftTeams**: This is the first cmdlet you need to execute in order to get access to the Microsoft Teams context of your tenant:

  (a) -TenantId <String>

  (b) -AccountId <String>

  (c) -TeamsEnvironmentName <String>

- **Disconnect-MicrosoftTeams**: After executing your cmdlets, you can close the connection to your tenant using this cmdlet.

To know the ID of your tenant, you can use the Connect cmdlet without passing any parameter. On the login popup, provide your organizational credentials and, after a few seconds, you will get the information pertaining to your tenant, as shown in the following screenshot:

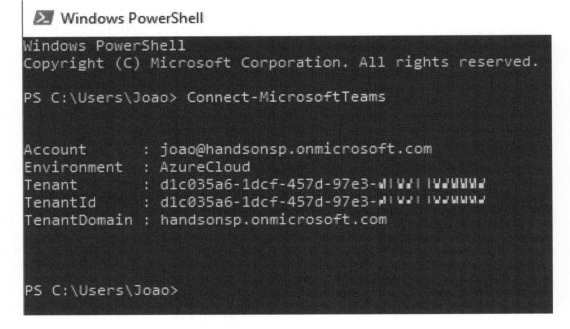

Figure 10.8: Tenant ID

Get cmdlets

The descriptions and parameters of the get cmdlets are as follows:

- **Get-Team:** This is used to get information about teams. It can get all the teams, archived teams, or even all the teams to which a user belongs:

    (a) `-GroupId <String>`

    (b) `-User <String>`

    (c) `-Archived <Boolean>`

    (d) `-Visibility <String>`

    (e) `-DisplayName <String>`

    (f) `-MailNickName <String>`

- **Get-TeamChannel**: This retrieves all the channels in the team:

    (a) `-GroupId <String>`

- **Get-TeamChannelUser**: This retrieves all the users of a channel, and it allows you to pre-filter users by role, that is, either **Owner** or **Member**:

    (a) `-GroupId <String>`

    (b) `-DisplayName <String>`

    (c) `-Role <String>`

- **Get-TeamsApp**: This returns the information pertaining to the apps installed in your tenant. The distribution method accepts as a parameter **Global** (apps from the store) or **Organization** (custom apps):

    (a) `-Id <String>`

    (b) `-ExternalId <String>`

    (c) `-DisplayName <String>`

    (d) `-DistributionMethod <String>`

- **Get-TeamUser:** This retrieves the user information from a team. It allows you to pre-filter users by role, that is, either **Owner** or **Member**:

    (a) `-GroupId <String>`

    (b) `-Role <String>`

Most of the Microsoft Teams cmdlets need to get the group ID as a parameter. This is the unique identifier from the Office group associated with the team. If you need to get the group ID of your team, execute the following cmdlet using the team name:

```
Get-Team -DisplayName "Project X"
```

From the result data, you will get the group ID as shown in the following screenshot:

Figure 10.9: Team details

Set cmdlets

The descriptions and parameters of the set cmdlets are as follows:

- **Set-Team**: This allows you to modify the settings of an existing team:

    (a) `-GroupId <String>`

    (b) `-DisplayName <String>`

    (c) `-Description <String>`

    (d) `-MailNickName <String>`

    (e) `-Classification <String>`

    (f) `-Visibility <String>`

    (g) `-AllowGiphy <Boolean>`

    (h) `-GiphyContentRating <String>`

    (i) `-AllowStickersAndMemes <Boolean>`

    (j) `-AllowCustomMemes <Boolean>`

    (k) `-AllowGuestCreateUpdateChannels <Boolean>`

    (l) `-AllowGuestDeleteChannels <Boolean>`

    (m) `-AllowCreateUpdateChannels <Boolean>`

    (n) `-AllowDeleteChannels <Boolean>`

(o) -AllowAddRemoveApps <Boolean>

(p) -AllowCreateUpdateRemoveTabs <Boolean>

(q) -AllowCreateUpdateRemoveConnectors <Boolean>

(r) -AllowUserEditMessages <Boolean>

(s) -AllowUserDeleteMessages <Boolean>

(t) -AllowOwnerDeleteMessages <Boolean>

(u) -AllowTeamMentions <Boolean>

(v) -AllowChannelMentions <Boolean>

(w) -ShowInTeamsSearchAndSuggestions <Boolean>

- **Set-TeamArchivedState**: This archives or unarchives a team. It can also make the SharePoint site read-only for members:

(a) -GroupId <False>

(b) -Archived <Boolean>

(c) -SetSpoSiteReadOnlyForMembers <Boolean>

- **Set-TeamChannel**: This allows you to modify the settings of an existing channel:

(a) -GroupId <String>

(b) -CurrentDisplayName <String>

(c) -NewDisplayName <String>

(d) -Description <String>

- **Set-TeamPicture**: This allows you to define the team picture for a team. The image path is the physical location of the image on your computer:

(a) -GroupId <String>

(b) -CurrentDisplayName <String>

(c) -NewDisplayName <String>

(d) -Description <String>

- **Set-TeamsApp**: This allows you to update a custom app already installed in your tenant. The path is the physical location of the app package on your computer, and the ID is the unique identifier of your app:

(a) -Id <String>

(b) -Path <String>

New cmdlets

The descriptions and parameters of the new cmdlets are as follows:

- **New-Team:** This allows you to create a new team and fill all the settings to apply by default with a single instruction:

(a) `-DisplayName <String>`

(b) `-Description <String>`

(c) `-MailNickName <String>`

(d) `-Classification <String>`

(e) `-Visibility <String>`

(f) `-Template <String>`

(g) `-Owner <String>`

(h) `-AllowGiphy <Boolean>`

(i) `-GiphyContentRating <Boolean>`

(j) `-AllowStickersAndMemes <Boolean>`

(k) `-AllowCustomMemes <Boolean>`

(l) `-AllowGuestCreateUpdateChannels <Boolean>`

(m) `-AllowGuestDeleteChannels <Boolean>`

(n) `-AllowCreateUpdateChannels <Boolean>`

(o) `-AllowDeleteChannels <Boolean>`

(p) `-AllowAddRemoveApps <Boolean>`

(q) `-AllowCreateUpdateRemoveTabs <Boolean>`

(r) `-AllowCreateUpdateRemoveConnectors <Boolean>`

(s) `-AllowUserEditMessages <Boolean>`

(t) `-AllowUserDeleteMessages <Boolean>`

(u) `-AllowOwnerDeleteMessages <Boolean>`

(v) `-AllowTeamMentions <Boolean>`

(w) `-AllowChannelMentions <Boolean>`

(x) `-ShowInTeamsSearchAndSuggestions <Boolean>`

- **New-TeamChannel**: This allows you to create a new channel and fill the default settings. The membership type is the parameter where you define whether the channel is **Public** or **Private**:

  (a) `-GroupId <String>`

  (b) `-DisplayName <String>`

  (c) `-Description <String>`

  (d) `-MembershipType <String>`

  (e) `-Owner <String>`

- **New-TeamsApp**: This allows you to install a custom app. The path is the physical location of the app package on your computer:

  (a) `-DistributionMethod <String>`

  (b) `-Path <String>`

Add cmdlets

The descriptions and parameters of the add cmdlets are as follows:

- **Add-TeamUser**: This adds a user to a team as a **Member** or **Owner**:

  (a) `-GroupId<String>`

  (b) `-User <String>`

  (c) `-Role <String>`

- **Add-TeamChannelUser**: This adds a user to a private channel as a **Member** or **Owner**:

  (a) `-GroupId <String>`

  (b) `-DisplayName <String>`

  (c) `-User <String>`

  (d) `-Role <String>`

Remove cmdlets

The descriptions and parameters of the remove cmdlets are as follows:

- **Remove-Team**: This removes a team and all its associated assets, including the SharePoint site collection and the Office group:

  (a) –GroupId <String>

- **Remove-TeamChannel**: This removes a channel from a team. The use of this cmdlet will not delete any of the documents relating to the channel. They will continue to exist in the team SharePoint site collection:

  (a) –GroupId <String>

  (b) –DisplayName <String>

- **Remove-TeamChannelUser**: This removes a user from a private channel:

  (a) -GroupId <String>

  (b) -DisplayName <String>

  (c) -User <String>

- **Remove-TeamsApp**: This removes an app from a team:

  (a) -Id <String>

- **Remove-TeamUser**: This removes a user from a team:

  (a) -GroupId <String>

  (b) -User <String>

  (c) -Role <String>

Even though Microsoft Teams provides its own PowerShell module, due to the legacy of the platform, there are things such as policies that are available through the use of the Skype for Business module, as we will see in the following section.

Installing the Skype for Business PowerShell Module

As mentioned several times during the book, operations related to policies need to be performed in batches of 20 users or through the use of PowerShell. The cmdlets included in the Microsoft Teams module do not support tasks related to policies. Those operations, however, can be executed using the Skype for Business PowerShell module.

The Skype for Business module is not available in the PowerShell gallery, which means it needs to be downloaded and installed manually. To do this, perform the following steps:

1. Open the Skype for Business download page: `https://www.microsoft.com/en-us/download/details.aspx?id=39366`.

2. Click on the **Download** button and select the location to save it on your computer.

3. Open the `.exe` file, agree with the terms and conditions, and then click on **Install**:

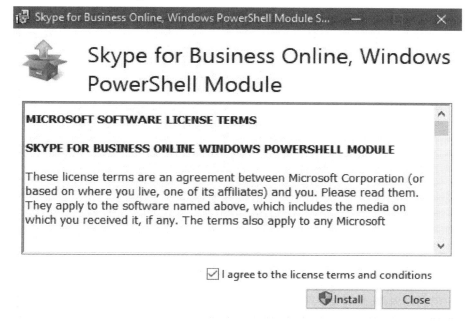

Figure 10.10: Installing the Skype for Business module

4. If you have a PowerShell session already opened, you need to close and restart it before using the module

What are the available cmdlets in the Skype for Business module?

The cmdlets included in the Skype for Business module have a different syntax to the ones included in the Microsoft Teams module. You can easily identify a Skype cmdlet by the *Cs* prefix in the name.

This module was not built specifically for Microsoft Teams, which means that most of the cmdlets are not supported by the application. In the following sections, you can find all the related cmdlets that allow you to work with Microsoft Teams policies.

> **Note: List of cmdlets**
>
> The Skype for Business PowerShell module includes more cmdlets than the ones described in this section. You can take a closer look at the entire list of cmdlets at the following address: `https://docs.microsoft.com/en-us/powershell/module/skype/?view=skype-ps`.

Get cmdlets

A description of each of the get cmdlets is as follows:

- **Get-CsTeamsAppSetupPolicy**: This gets all the app setup policies in the tenant with the IDs of the pinned apps.
- **Get-CsTeamsCallingPolicy**: This gets all the calling policies in the tenant with all the associated settings.
- **Get-CsTeamsChannelsPolicy**: This gets all the policies defined for the channels.
- **Get-CsTeamsMeetingPolicy**: This gets all the meeting policies and their settings.
- **Get-CsTeamsMessagingPolicy**: This gets all the messaging policies and their settings.

Grant cmdlets

A description of each of the grant cmdlets is as follows:

- **Grant-CsTeamsAppPermissionPolicy**: This applies an app permission policy to a single user:

  (a) `-Identity <String>`

  (b) `-PolicyName <String>`

  (c) `-PassThru <SwitchParameter>`

  (d) `-WhatIf <SwitchParameter>`

- **Grant-CsTeamsAppSetupPolicy**: This applies an app setup policy to a single user:
  (a) `-Identity <String>`
  (b) `-PolicyName <String>`
  (c) `-PassThru <SwitchParameter>`
  (d) `-WhatIf <SwitchParameter>`

- **Grant-CsTeamsCallingPolicy**: This applies a calling permission policy to a single user:
  (a) `-Identity <String>`
  (b) `-PolicyName <String>`
  (c) `-PassThru <SwitchParameter>`
  (d) `-WhatIf <SwitchParameter>`

- **Grant-CsTeamsChannelsPolicy**: This applies a channel policy to a single user:
  (a) `-Identity <String>`
  (b) `-PolicyName <String>`
  (c) `-PassThru <SwitchParameter>`
  (d) `-WhatIf <SwitchParameter>`

- **Grant-CsTeamsMeetingPolicy**: This applies a meeting policy to a single user:
  (a) `-Identity <String>`
  (b) `-PolicyName <String>`
  (c) `-PassThru <SwitchParameter>`
  (d) `-WhatIf <SwitchParameter>`

- **Grant-CsTeamsMessagingPolicy**: This applies a messaging policy to a single user:
  (a) `-Identity <String>`
  (b) `-PolicyName <String>`
  (c) `-PassThru <SwitchParameter>`
  (d) `-WhatIf <SwitchParameter>`

New cmdlets

A description of each of the new cmdlets is as follows:

- **New-CsTeamsChannelsPolicy**: This creates a new channel policy:

  (a) `-Identity <String>`

  (b) `-AllowOrgWideTeamCreation <Boolean>`

  (c) `-AllowPrivateTeamDiscovery <Boolean>`

  (d) `-AllowPrivateChannelCreation <Boolean>`

- **New-CsTeamsMeetingPolicy**: This creates a new meeting policy:

  (a) `-Identity <String>`

  (b) `-Description <String>`

  (c) `-AllowChannelMeetingScheduling <Boolean>`

  (d) `-AllowMeetNow <Boolean>`

  (e) `-AllowIPVideo <Boolean>`

  (f) `-AllowAnonymousUsersToDialOut <Boolean>`

  (g) `-AllowAnonymousUsersToStartMeeting <Boolean>`

  (h) `-AllowPrivateMeetingScheduling <Boolean>`

  (i) `-AutoAdmittedUsers <String>`

  (j) `-AllowCloudRecording <Boolean>`

  (k) `-AllowOutlookAddIn <Boolean>`

  (l) `-AllowPowerPointSharing <Boolean>`

  (m) `-AllowParticipantGiveRequestControl <Boolean>`

  (n) `-AllowExternalParticipantGiveRequestControl <Boolean>`

  (o) `-AllowSharedNotes <Boolean>`

  (p) `-AllowWhiteboard <Boolean>`

  (q) `-AllowTranscription <Boolean>`

  (r) `-MediaBitRateKb <UInt32>`

  (s) `-ScreenSharingMode <String>`

- **New-CsTeamsMessagingPolicy**: This creates a new messaging policy:

  (a) `-Identity <String>`

  (b) `-AllowOwnerDeleteMessage <Boolean>`

  (c) `-Description <String>`

  (d) `-AllowUserChat <Boolean>`

  (e) `-AllowStickers <Boolean>`

  (f) `-AllowUrlPreviews <Boolean>`

  (g) `-AllowImmersiveReader <Boolean>`

  (h) `-AllowUserTranslation <Boolean>`

  (i) `-AllowUserEditMessage <Boolean>`

  (j) `-AllowRemoveUser <Boolean>`

  (k) `-ReadReceiptsEnabledType <String>`

  (l) `-AllowMemes <Boolean>`

  (m) `-AllowPriorityMessages <Boolean>`

  (n) `-GiphyRatingType <String>`

  (o) `-AllowGiphy <Boolean>`

Remove cmdlets

A description of each of the remove cmdlets is as follows:

- **Remove-CsTeamsAppPermissionPolicy**: This removes an app permission policy:

  (a) `-Tenant <String>`

  (b) `-Identity <String>`

- **Remove-CsTeamsAppSetupPolicy**: This removes an app setup policy:

  (a) `-Tenant <String>`

  (b) `-Identity <String>`

- **Remove-CsTeamsChannelsPolicy**: This removes a channel permission policy:

  (a) `-Tenant <String>`

  (b) `-Identity <String>`

- **Remove-CsTeamsMeetingPolicy**: This removes a meeting policy:

  (a) `-Tenant <String>`

  (b) `-Identity <String>`

- **Remove-CsTeamsMessagingPolicy**: This removes a messaging policy:

  (a) `-Tenant <String>`

  (b) `-Identity <String>`

Combining Microsoft Teams and Skype for Business PowerShell modules allows you to automate pretty much all the administrative tasks you will have to implement with Microsoft Teams. In the following section, you will learn from examples how to build your own scripts.

Learning how to use PowerShell from examples

In this section of the book, you will find four examples of how PowerShell can be used to automate tasks within Microsoft Teams and the script used to solve each of the scenarios.

The code includes comments so that you can follow along with what is happening. Comments are identified by a hashtag (#). For better readability of the code, the comments only include a number, while the comment description is provided after the code section.

Example 1: Victor

Victor is the IT guy in his company and oftentimes, his colleagues ask him to create teams according to internal policies and conventions. To avoid doing this task manually over and over again, Victor has created a PowerShell script. This includes the following:

1. Team settings.

2. Team default channels.

3. Team default members.

4. Establishing a connection to Microsoft Teams: Using this cmdlet without parameters will open a login popup and will authenticate you in your organization tenant.

5. Team creation: The result is saved to a variable to use the group ID in the following instructions.

6. Channel creation: This loops through the channel list to create the channel. The group ID was saved in the `New-Team` instruction.

7. Adding default members to the team: This loops through the array of users and adds them to the team as members.

The following script and corresponding numbers show how Victor would do this:

```
#1
$teamName= "Project Y"
$teamDescription= "The new generation of electric skateboards"
$teamOwner= "joao@funskating.com"
$teamVisibility= "Private"
$teamEditMessagesPolicy= $false
$teamDeliteMessagesPolicy= $false


#2
$teamChannels= @("Procedures", "Legal")


#3
$teamMembers= @("josh@funskating.com", "adele@funskating.com")


#4
Connect-MicrosoftTeams


#5
$teamDetails=New-Team -DisplayName $teamName -Description
$teamDescription -Owner $teamOwner -Visibility $teamVisibility
-AllowUserEditMessages $teamEditMessagesPolicy
-AllowOwnerDeleteMessages $teamDeliteMessagesPolicy


#6
for ($i=0; $i-lt$teamChannels.length; $i++) {
    New-TeamChannel -GroupId $teamDetails.GroupId -DisplayName
$teamChannels[$i]
}


#7
```

```
for ($i=0; $i-lt$teamMembers.length; $i++) {
    Add-TeamUser -GroupId$teamDetails.GroupId
-User$teamMembers[$i] -role"Member"
}


Disconnect-MicrosoftTeams
```

Example 2: John

John is heading up several projects in his company that are spread across the globe. Each project is assigned to a country and has its own team on Microsoft Teams. John wants to create a channel in each one of his teams where he can communicate the procedures for each country and where people can communicate about this topic. The script includes the following:

1. Establishing a team owner and a new channel name definition.

2. Connecting to Microsoft Teams and getting all the teams to which the user belongs. This will include those teams where the user is an owner and member.

3. Looping through all the teams

4. Getting the current team group ID and the list of owners.

5. Looping through the owners of the team.

6. Comparing the current owner of the team with the email defined at the top of the script. If the condition is true, this means that the current team is owned by John and a new channel is then created on it.

The following script and corresponding numbers show how John would do this:

```
#1
$teamOwnerEmail= "john@funskating.com"
$channelName= "Projects"


#2
Connect-MicrosoftTeams
$teamsWhereIam = Get-Team -User $teamOwner


#3
for ($i=0; $i-lt $teamsWhereIam.length; $i++) {
    #4
```

```
        $groupId= $teamsWhereIam[$i].GroupId
        $teamOwners=Get-TeamUser -GroupId $groupId -Role Owner
        #5
        for ($j=0; $j-lt$teamOwners.length; $j++) {
            #6
            if($teamOwners[$j].User -eq $teamOwnerEmail){
                    New-TeamChannel -GroupId $groupId -DisplayName
$channelName
            }
        }
    }
Disconnect-MicrosoftTeams
```

Example 3: The Funny Company

The Funny Company has a very informal culture and wants to make sure that this is reflected on Microsoft Teams. From now on, all teams should have all the fun settings on. The script will do the following:

1. Connect to Microsoft Teams.

2. Get all teams.

3. Loop through all teams.

4. Get each team group ID and define the fun settings.

The following script and corresponding numbers show how the Funny Company would do this:

```
#1
Connect-MicrosoftTeams

#2
$allTeams= Get-Team

#3
for ($i=0; $i-lt$allTeams.length; $i++) {
    #4
    $groupId=$allTeams[$i].GroupId
```

```
    Set-Team -GroupId $groupId -AllowGiphy $true -
GiphyContentRating moderate -AllowStickersAndMemes $true -
AllowCustomMemes $true
}


Disconnect-MicrosoftTeams
```

Example 4: Hugh

Hugh is the Microsoft Teams administrator at his company and is responsible for managing all policies. Recently, he has installed a global app where all the company news and announcements are published. Even though the adoption of Microsoft Teams is great, users are not using the new app, mainly because it is hidden in the More apps menu. To increase adoption of the app, Hugh wants to apply a new policy to all users where the company app is the first one listed in the app bar. The script will include the following:

1. Authentication using the Skype for Business PowerShell module. This process will open a windows authentication popup where you must insert your credentials:

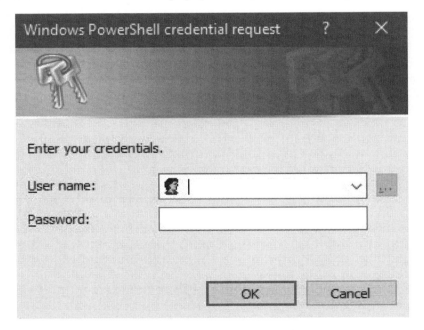

Figure 10.11: Authentication window

2. User definitions: This is the list of users to whom the new app setup policy will be applied.

3. Looping thorough the list of users and applying the company app policy.

The following script and corresponding numbers show how Hugh would do this:

```
#1
Import-ModuleSkypeOnlineConnector
$credentials= Get-Credential
$sfbSession= New-CsOnlineSession -Credential $credentials
Import-PSSession $sfbSession


#2
$usersEmails= @("peter@funskating.com","maria@funskating.com")


#3
for ($i=0; $i-lt$usersEmails.length; $i++) {
    Grant-CsTeamsAppSetupPolicy -identity $usersEmails[$i]
-PolicyName "Company App"
}
```

You can use these simple scenarios as a starting point for automating tasks on Microsoft Teams. This will save you a lot of time while ensuring consistency across all your teams and policies.

Summary

In this chapter, you have learned how you can automate processes on Microsoft Teams using the PowerShell modules. After this chapter, you should be able to build your PowerShell scripts to automate the administrative tasks you need to perform in your organization.

This book gave you a global overview of what Microsoft Teams is by covering all the basic features and concepts.

As you progressed into the book, it became more technical and gave you an overview of how things can be configured as an end user or as an admin. Finally, you learned how to achieve more by extending Teams and automating processes.

Now, you should be the real hero of Microsoft Teams in your organization and you are ready to empower others to achieve more using this awesome platform.

Thank you,

João Ferreira

Other Books You May Enjoy

If you enjoyed this book, you may be interested in these other books by Packt:

Microsoft 365 Certified Fundamentals MS-900 Exam Guide

Aaron Guilmette, Marcos Zanre, and Yura Lee

ISBN: 978-1-83898-217-1

- Gain insights into the exam objectives, test scenarios, and knowledge required before taking the MS-900 exam

- Understand the cloud services and SaaS models available in the Microsoft ecosystem

- Identify Windows deployment considerations using the Admin Center and User Portal experiences

- Implement enterprise mobility, device management, and application management within your organization

- Explore the reporting and analytics capabilities of Microsoft 365

- Discover various features of Azure Active Directory and other Microsoft 365 security tools

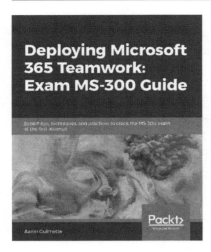

Deploying Microsoft 365 Teamwork: Exam MS-300 Guide

Aaron Guilmette

ISBN: 978-1-83898-773-2

- Discover the different Microsoft services and features that make up Office 365

- Configure cloud services for your environment and extend your infrastructure's capabilities

- Understand site architecture, site settings, and hub settings in SharePoint Online

- Explore business connectivity services for view and access options in SharePoint Online

- Configure Yammer to integrate with Office 365 groups, SharePoint, and Teams

- Deploy SharePoint Online, OneDrive for Business, and Microsoft Teams successfully, including bots and connectors

Leave a review - let other readers know what you think

Please share your thoughts on this book with others by leaving a review on the site that you bought it from. If you purchased the book from Amazon, please leave us an honest review on this book's Amazon page. This is vital so that other potential readers can see and use your unbiased opinion to make purchasing decisions, we can understand what our customers think about our products, and our authors can see your feedback on the title that they have worked with Packt to create. It will only take a few minutes of your time, but is valuable to other potential customers, our authors, and Packt. Thank you!

Index

Printed in Great Britain
by Amazon